D1637167

ADRIENNE VON SPEYR

The Victory of Love

ADRIENNE VON SPEYR

The Victory of Love

A Meditation on Romans 8

Foreword by
Hans Urs von Balthasar

Translated by Sister Lucia Wiedenhöver, O.C.D.

IGNATIUS PRESS   SAN FRANCISCO

Title of the German original:
Der Sieg der Liebe:
Betrachtung über Romer 8
© 1953 Johannes Verlag, Einsiedeln

Cover by Joan McGrady Beach

© 1990 Ignatius Press, San Francisco
ISBN 0-89870-304-2
Library of Congress catalogue number 90-81773
Printed in the United States of America

CONTENTS

FOREWORD

The eighth chapter of the Letter to the Romans is such a radiant, blasting trumpet-call in the tremendous symphony of the Pauline writings that we may let its message have its effect on us even when taken out of the context of the Letter. Such concentration on parts of Scripture, as practiced continually by the Church in her liturgy and proclamation, is a new reminder of how much the Word of God, though horizontally bound up with humanity and history, pierces down vertically from Heaven at every point and that it must be accepted by man in nakedness of heart without safety measures and escape routes. The theme of this chapter is the ultimate victory of the love of God the Father through Christ in the Holy Spirit in the faithful united as the Church, brothers and coheirs of the Son. Through the Church also the whole of creation calling out for redemption attains its ultimate freedom. Nothing can hold back the constant extension of this victory or prevent the progress of this triumphal train. It is impossible to cut short Saint Paul's words by putting limits to their meaning. His proclamation has here the character of

7

absolute though progressive totality. Not to have recognized this was the error of those heretics who wanted to find in the final verses a confirmation of their subjective consciousness of being saved, on the basis of an unbiblical doctrine of predestination that sets individuals against other individuals. Adrienne von Speyr avoids this trap, as she already avoided the first one of limiting the Apostle's words from outside. In keeping with her usual procedure, she remains within the pure unadulterated objectivity of the work of redemption and its application. She does not allow herself to use the term "election" outside the context of salvation-history, therefore as the obligatory imposition of a mission. According to her, this is the biblical, Old Testament, as well as especially Pauline and Johannine, meaning of the mystery of election.

From unpublished material of the author I quote a text that belongs here:

> When Paul speaks of the elect he means definite individuals. He sees before his eyes the image of the disciples who followed the Lord: they are types and models, the central light falls on them. That this light falls from them on to others, is brought by them to others, is a new truth not excluded but included in the first. At first Peter is intended, or John, and not Zebedee, though he stands near the circle of light. The number itself is the Son's secret. It could be that the Father means "many" and that, to speak in a human way, he allows himself to be surprised by the work of the Son who demands "all". Little Thérèse

8

"chose all" when she was offered a basketful of things to choose from. She chose not only what was beautiful but also the unattractive. Thérèse is only imitating what is the deepest in the attitude of the Son of Man: he was the first "to choose all", even the last human being in the basket of creation, perhaps unrecognizable because of sin, but beautiful because the Father created him.

We have no right to fix prematurely the dimensions of the mysterious work of the Son. But wherever the beams of the sun of grace shine with special splendor, we should not avert our faces in false bashfulness but bow in reverent gratitude before the gift.

In this age, which has fallen in love with the darker sides of man, the Christian needs nothing more urgently than the courage to turn to the divine light. In an age that attempts to attain the total self-sufficiency of a world closed in upon itself, he is called to transcend this vainly attempted ideal through a completely different, victorious totality of redemption. In contrast to our age, we see revealed, with larger horizons than perhaps were ever visible before, how immeasurable are the treasures of God's grace.

Hans Urs von Balthasar

I

THE SEPARATION

1. There is now therefore no condemnation for them that are in Christ Jesus.

Now signifies the moment from which the new becomes apparent. Not timidly, not creepingly, not just anyhow. It appears with the force of a fresh spring, with the absoluteness of a perfect truth, streaming forth, overflowing. With the freshness of the present moment just born. But also with the experience and certainty of a Now that has known struggle, that leaves something behind, puts an ending to something. In this end lies the beginning. And the beginning is that nothing exists deserving *condemnation*. Everything is blotted out. The Now does however include a relationship to the past that it resolves within the new beginning. The experience of the past is perfectly present in order to give way totally to the new truth. In being swallowed up it is being used to accelerate the birth of the new moment. The rise of that moment is like the sunrise when the night is over; it *is* over because the sun is risen. The past *is* over because the Now is here; the past experience *is* left behind because the new has begun. It has entered into the present Now. The scaffolding is being removed so that the outlines of the new house become fully visible; the house is strong enough to stand without the scaffolding. Now there is *nothing deserving condemnation*, rejection, nothing that could evoke blame, misgivings or justified hesitation, because there is but *one* truth surpassing all other truths: *Christ*. The truth is "Christ". And whoever is *in* him is in the truth, is not being tested by anything outside, cannot be vanquished, reduced to silence, replaced by anything else, or displaced, cannot be regarded as a side-issue. Whoever is *in Christ Jesus* is in the source, is in the truth. He is bathed by it, molded and nourished by it. As long as he was not in the source he was something indifferent: perhaps something atrophying, pining away, dying. His being was inessential. What he did was not done in the truth. From the standpoint of the truth it was despicable and could not be regarded as good and genuine. Now everything in the believer is good and genuine because it rests in the light, in the truth. He is renewed, and the renewal is love's. The renewal does not take place in such a way that the transformation makes him unrecognizable. He is not something today that has nothing to do with what he will be tomorrow.

Today and tomorrow meet in the Now. Only yesterday is left behind. What deserves condemnation is left far behind, like a garment one has taken off, a skin no longer used. It is something that once was judged and now no longer has any right to exist. The believer looked at it before as belonging to him, but in the meantime he has recognized it as false and ungenuine and has now nothing more to do with it. The Now contains an Over. What was before is over. But the incompleteness of the new man in the Lord shows that the borderlines have been moved: it is no longer man seeking for some law to live by, some truth to conform to, some direction in which to walk. He has been assigned a place, the place where the Lord is waiting for him. It is as if Christ stood there with arms outstretched to take him to his heart and give him the place of preference, that of the Beloved Disciple; to draw him to that place where Christ can do something with him. He has no wish to make use of him in order to have done with him. Nor does he want to invent new customs, a new law to give a suitable framework to this man in his insufficiency. The Lord needs him because he has made him a part of his truth. Because he has taken him into himself, into the hiddenness of his own being. Man now has a home, a place from where he can do together with Christ what he is called to do. The Lord does not try to weaken him or muffle his effectiveness. He is not out to fight for his own rights and constantly to stress the distance between God and man or on the basis of faith to threaten man's security regarding his own achievement. He gives him an unlimited share in his own achievement as Redeemer, in his own effectiveness and being. Because this place is Christ himself, every yardstick is surpassed. Who could measure the Lord, evaluate him, divide his work into partial achievements that can be counted up? When the Son shows himself on earth in the revelation of the Triune God, he speaks words of ultimate and immeasurable greatness.

"He who sees me sees the Father." His very origin negates every limiting measure. Their commonality and being is stressed, the Trinity is expressed in the unity. Something similar happens also with the man who is in Christ. As long as something that was to be condemned existed in him, it was necessary to measure and draw limits; this weighing was not only necessary, it was a strict commandment. But now he can be in the Lord, and to be in him means abiding and remaining in him. It is a completely new form of being. Who could measure eternal Being by his passage through passing time! Who could try to catch the length of eternity by counting days, epochs and periods of time! So the meaning of what is condemned and the truth of what is rejected is past, for in Jesus Christ there is room for everything except sin.

2. *For the law of the Spirit of life in Christ Jesus has set me free from the law of sin and death.*

The Now of the previous verse shines out once more. It is a different moment. There was the law with death as consequence, law leading to death, because everything was determined by sin, and sin alone remained visible. Since the time of the Fall sin and death coincide. Sin leads to death, and the law was the expression of their connection as cause and effect. When the Apostle speaks of this his readers realize that they know this law, that they had been subject to it. This law had been normal and entirely logical to them. And now he says of himself that he is free of the law. They know him, they know his past, they are linked to him. This man whom they know stands beyond the law in the freedom of one who has overcome. This victory was achieved within a new *law of the Spirit* so strong that it sets free at once. It is so new that it overcomes what is old, so full of grace that punishment disappears. It is a law of the Spirit, the Spirit which is *life*. Spirit and life form a closely knit unity presenting a power in contrast to the power of sin and death.

This power breaks through the law hitherto valid, but not to make compromises with rules and exceptions; nor in such a way that those walking in the new law have to continue to look back to the old in order not to break it or infringe anyone's right. No, the new law is victorious because it means life *in Christ Jesus* and because it *sets free* in him. Suddenly there shines out from the whole statement of the Apostle the One who has brought the law of the Spirit and overcome death. It is clear that Christ has vanquished death through his death and Resurrection, yes, through the unity of death and Resurrection. But it is new that he should have created a law of freedom that overcomes the law of death. The Lord thus appears as lawgiver. He does not simply follow in the old footsteps in order to fulfill the promises, but he has created something new. He has fulfilled them, but he brought his own law of life with him, life in his Spirit, a spirit in his life. He has become the key figure of the new law, even the lawgiver himself who creates something new and abolishes the old with this new creation. Those who live in him will need no other law than his. Thus he lives in us and among us in order to share everything with us. He took our flesh, but gave us his Spirit. It is like creating a counterbalance to the Incarnation. He borrowed from us our humanity. He lived it humanly, perfectly, as one in our midst. He gave us his Eucharist: the continuance of his being flesh and blood. And he brought as counterpiece a law of the Spirit which he shares with those who live in his life not only through his life, but are found right in himself. We knew a life of sin; it led to death. Now we know a life of the Spirit; it leads to life, endless life, because it is life in Christ, and Christ possesses eternal life. We can now exchange our life, the finite for the infinite, the perishable for the eternal, law for law. New light falls on human freedom from here. It remains freedom under a law, not the law that tends to death, but the law that contains life, a life of the Spirit, an enlarged life. Enlarged not only as to its length but also to its breadth: its space is the eternal space of the Lord. Man is set free for this greater life. The law does not bind, it liberates man, analogous to an absolution. Saint Paul could have spoken in the same way about the Sacrament of Confession, which liberated from sin in order to make us share through absolution in the life of the Eternal, the life of the Lord.

The believer receives a new conception of the law. He receives at the same time a new conception of life. For the liberation from a life of sin leads to life under a law, but it is the law of one living in Christ. It means a real sharing in life, in the Spirit, in the Lord. The body with its demands and temptations, its perishability and misery, appears to take second place. The Spirit is Spirit of life, Holy Spirit, Spirit of God, urgently asked for and bestowed; Spirit brought by the Son, after the Spirit brought the Son to earth. It is a gift returned. The Spirit overshadowed the Mother and brought about the Incarnation of the Son. But the Son now makes the Spirit the principle of life in him. The Spirit brought the Son to us as one who wants to live with us. Now the Son brings us the Spirit so that we may live: in the Son and the Spirit.

3. For God has done what the law, weakened by the flesh, could not do: sending his own Son in the likeness of sinful flesh and for sin, he condemned sin in the flesh.

The law hitherto followed now appears in all its limitation, and Paul here stresses this fact only. It was powerless, has limits beyond which it could not lead because the limitation was that of death. Law and death correspond to each other insofar as the law found its application wherever there was sin, and sin led to death. Death on its part was contained in the law and bound the law to itself. In death, an end was foreseen to the law, the life according to the law was limited to time. It was a weak life because it bore death in itself. The law was incapable of bringing liberation. Therefore *God sent his Son* into the world thus marked by law, sin and death. He allowed his Son to become man *in the likeness of sinful flesh*. In order to be one among us, the Son of Man evidently was not to appear different from us. Anyone seeing him might think him subject to the law like the rest of us. But this was only a *likeness*. The Son was God and became man in order to overcome the law, to set it free from its *being weakened by the flesh* and give to humanity the freedom of life and of the Spirit which he himself possesses in such abundance that he had enough for everyone, and everyone could live in him, with him, together.

The Father had *condemned sin* from the beginning. In this condemnation of sin his great love for men was hidden from the beginning, the original love of the Creator for his creatures. And in order to show them this love effectively he had to give them life there where it was most effectively at work: in his Son. So he has sent the Son into the world for the same reason for which he had to condemn sin: to bring about a separation and the possibility of a new law with the power of abolishing death.

In committing sin, man had made the attempt of distancing himself from God. But God is able to adopt human nature in order to retrieve man back.

Perhaps man felt very threatened by the old law but did not have the strength to overcome it. He continued in sin, became a victim of the law and had to die. And now there is a man who does not commit sin, will never do so, who lives outside the law not as one outlawed, but as embodying the new law. He inaugurates it, is the bearer of it, shares it out at the price of his own life, which he does not defend. He lavishes it away, shares it out for the price of his own being, which he does not keep closed. He opens it so that all may find room in it, live in it, move in it and feel at home. Because in the Son there is no room for sin, there is in him no room for death, either. And because in him there is no room for death, there is no possibility of condemnation. Everything finds its solution, not through mankind being abandoned, but by being restored to its home. Man is submitted to the new law of the Son, is permitted to live in loving him. The distance from the Father is bridged over by the Son. In him it ceases to exist. This means that one who lives in the Son of Man enjoys the Father's friendship and is untouched by condemnation.

God the Father did not merely acquiesce in this, he willed it. He sent the Son, and in this mission is contained life, spirit and new law. Condemnation is put at a distance because it is connected with the law that leads to death. The Father no longer looks for man in this law; he looks for him in the Son and finds him there, under the law of the Son. The new beginning, which is liberation, remains in the Son.

God gives to the second Adam flesh that is similar

to the flesh of the first Adam, flesh that failed in the first Adam and has continued to fail throughout generations. It experiences temptations and does not resist them; perhaps it creates temptations itself. Death was the most painful punishment for this flesh, because man who loved sin could not bear the knowledge of its future consequence, for death put an end to temptation and sin without vanquishing them. And now the Son appears in flesh similar to this flesh, and God condemns sin in this flesh. He cannot punish a sin the Son might have committed in his flesh, for the Son does not sin. He remains God in the majesty of the divine when contrasted with what is human, but also in the lowliness of one become man. His flesh is unsullied. It is therefore suited to receive the paternal condemnation; the Son himself shares in this condemnation, not from Heaven, but on earth, in himself. He pays the price of this condemnation, this judgment, this justice achieved, on the Cross. On the Cross the condemnation of sin becomes visible. The flesh takes sin upon itself; in a larger sense it does this already in the Incarnation of the Son. If the flesh had not had such an important role in creation, in the Fall, in the Incarnation, God would have been able to punish somehow from Heaven. Sin would have been here and punishment there, man here and God there. But since the Son became man and one flesh with us and a man among us, no distinction can be made between Son of God and Son of Man, or between punishment and free acceptance of the responsibility for sin.

The Son allows his love to become the melting pot of condemnation, out of which redemption comes forth. Redemption is a new birth in the flesh of the Son. It cannot be said that condemnation and absolution could be distinguished as two separate phases, though they are closely linked together. Rather it is one indistinguishable whole and includes the entire earthly existence of the Son. The different phases melt into one, all dates fall together: the birth with the Cross, the Cross with the Resurrection. Everything is there united to pay the price the Father demands and to give to humanity a flesh that is pure and able to overcome every sin in itself. It is a gift of life, in which no death lies hidden. Death is vanquished. In this gift the purity and divinity of the Son has room to receive every sin. It is not a shortened process or a chance approximation. It is the radiant completeness in which even the last remnant of sin finds its place. The Son takes notice of every sin in order to redeem it. He does not disregard or overlook a single one in order to exclude it. Each is painful enough for him to be accepted and suffered for. Whoever hears the word "condemnation" from the Father knows about the inexorability of justice, its absolute claim that is waiting to be drawn forth to the light of day. There is a tremendous force in this condemnation, powerful enough to strike every sin. And so the human body of the Son in its weakness, in its failure to bear up any longer at the moment of death, must become the object of condemnation; it must become weak enough to receive this whole force, near enough to death in order to guarantee the genuineness of new life. The victory can be achieved only through death. In the death of the Son every sin must die. He brings it to its end. As long as sin was alive there was no room for the life of redemption. The new life demands every space, so that every space must be emptied for it.

4. *In order that the just requirement of the law might be fulfilled in us, who walk not according to the flesh but according to the Spirit.*

In us the just demands of the law shall be fulfilled; through the eucharistic Body of the Lord in us, within a new world, within a new kind of existence. "*In us*" means now a center. We are not the center ourselves, we are incapable of this. The Lord represents the center by becoming one of us, bearing in himself the condemnation of the flesh through the Father. He carries a new law in himself, and also its fulfillment that he brings wherever he goes. The Son touches us, lavishes himself upon us through his Eucharist and his Word; he gives us a center in which the Father can work. The Father recognizes in us the face of the Son. He sees us as new vessels waiting for the divine content. He sees us made obedient through the obedience of the Son, because the Son lives in us. In this way we become a center for the fulfillment, for something that is coming into existence and is accomplished by the Father. And what comes into existence is the *justice of the law*: something complete and perfect, thought out by God the Father and achieved by God the Son. The law is no longer in contrast to us. The law accepted and kept is not outside of us. It is satisfied in us. This means: we are relied upon as members of the Church of the Son, we are counted upon as the center of the Son's action. Through the Son we learn to *walk not according to the flesh but according to the Spirit*, as though the Son through his Eucharist had silenced our whole flesh. He brought about in us a movement toward himself, an acceptance of the new flesh, an agreement not only with his Incarnation and his whole life, but also with everything he wants to do in us, an agreement which is at once a deed, an effect, a surrender, a taking on of new tasks. We, too, begin to walk, we walk in the Spirit, in the Holy Spirit who can prescribe the new law and take care of its fulfillment.

God the Father, the Son and the Holy Spirit use our being in order to make real in our midst what they have planned and made real in Heaven: something new, a promising new beginning of life. The condition is faith. Faith in the new teaching. This faith is witnessed to by the fact that we walk in the Spirit. And this deed is accomplished by God and man together: by grace and with merit, because God the Father has condemned sin in the flesh of the Son. He has created this central point where we are freed from the burden of our flesh. The condemnation is no longer in us, it is taken outside of us, to another place. In its place the justice of the Father is fulfilled in our midst, it is now the justice of the new law. And so we walk within this new law that cannot be divided, we walk in the Spirit, the Holy Spirit. A whole series of developments takes place in order to bring about the one thing. If we look closely, we see these developments are all the consequence of the Son's Incarnation. The last consequence is at the same time the first, because the Son desired this particular redemption by creating this center in us. It belongs to the fulfillment of his cry: "It is consummated" that we have now been counted worthy to have this center of action within us.

5. For those who live according to the flesh set their minds on the things of the flesh, but those who live according to the Spirit set their minds on the things of the Spirit.

Flesh and Spirit are being separated; they form two poles apart. They are not absolutely torn apart, for they meet as two poles within man. Man is flesh and spirit; in his concrete existence he has the choice between flesh and spirit, so that either the one or the other will predominate. This statement receives its full meaning through the one made previously: through the Incarnation of the Son who assumes flesh in order that the Father may condemn sin in his flesh and in order that he as Son of Love and as Word of the Father may prove the predominance of the spirit in his Incarnation without doing away with the flesh, without revealing God only in Heaven, as Spirit. But the meaning of his Incarnation, of his Cross and of his death, points toward spirit. The flesh is subject to the spirit in such a way that spirit triumphs over the flesh and over any spirit that is not his Spirit. And the new law is a law of the Spirit.

Man, uniting both flesh and spirit, chooses between the two, rarely once and for all; most often he constantly rechooses; rarely in the spirit of the purity of the Lord, most often in his own spirit to which knowledge has been given but which remains constantly burdened with the weight of the flesh. A person who has once and for all overcome the flesh is so close to the Lord that he can only be a saint. The indestructible, indivisible truth that lives in the Lord is so strong, powerful and relevant that anyone who has grasped it will be free from every untruthfulness, including that of his own flesh. For the Christian who seriously follows Christ is part of the primal truth that the Son became man and that the Father condemned sin in him. This truth can (and must, if the discipleship is genuine) receive such a weight that it produces in the disciple the strength to strive after *the things of the spirit*, to love them, to allow himself to be penetrated by them, so that in every choice the Spirit is also chosen; the Spirit who leads to the Son who bears within himself the Father's condemnation of sin.

Flesh and spirit represent two worlds. The world of the flesh is the ego-world, the world of limitation, of selfish choice, of drawing all things to oneself, of the satisfaction and kindling of desires that are only functions of self. It is the glorification of one's own opportunities; play with a world that the man of the flesh thinks he is constantly creating without noticing that the center of this world remains static. He seeks variety and finds ever again only himself. In all the ecstasies he believes he is experiencing in what is new, he sees the old face of the ego reappear. It is therefore the world of everlasting constriction, of a confinement that narrows down into himself like a spiral movement. The world of the spirit is the world of the Divine Spirit, an eternal, infinite world. If there is a spiral movement in it, it is turned outside in infinite enlargement, forming circles each one of which surpasses the one before. And every occupation with the world of the spirit opens greater horizons. The ego is lost sight of and becomes ever more inessential, for everything is turned to the Son, everything becomes new and spiritual. At the end the flesh is related to the spirit no longer like a smaller subject power to a greater ruling one, but it becomes a likeness of the spirit in its service. This is not a denial of God's creation but a confirmation of the recapitulation of the world through the Son. Because the Father created man before the Son had brought home the world—although in Heaven it was already recapitulated, brought home—he left man the freedom of choice. But together with this freedom and in order to reveal its nature more clearly, God offers him the new law. This law does not have a face that is unknown: it bears the face of the crucified and the risen Lord, the face of Christmas, but also of the Ascension to the Father. If we are really trying to see God with the eyes of faith we will choose spirit. We will then see God one day, for we have entered the way of eternity, the way of God's life, the way that is marked by companionship with the Son.

6. *To set the mind on the flesh is death, but to set the mind on the Spirit is life and peace.*

The mind of the flesh is a closed circle in which man encloses himself, making himself the center of it. It is drawn through a number of points and around himself; each point is a certain reference to his self-love, desire for his own gratification, enjoyment and satisfaction. This satisfaction has in each case self for its object but also its subject. And the circle is drawn not just around man as a periphery to make up his world, but from each point it sends a ray to the center that is self. Direct and indirect rays. Not only the shortest way from each point to the center, but also from one point to the other; the other point then becomes a circuit in order to prolong the enjoyment and reach the center more surely. Perhaps this someone thinks he has made himself more secure by placing himself thus in the center. He was clever enough to direct all the lines of the circle back to himself; no opportunity is lost for enjoying himself in his own way. But the flesh is perishable; all the circles from flesh to flesh are circles of death. One has no

27

other end but himself; and this is not in a way that relates to God, entrusted to him and lifted up to him, but entrusted only to self: flesh in the flesh, together with the flesh, and thus marked with the sign of death. It does not matter if the wheel is turned and the opportunities are different ones—it remains death, inescapably. Suddenly the outward rim of the circle is turned inside and man sees with horror the death-markings facing him. Everything he constructed so carefully has been consigned to death, perhaps so thoroughly as to have hastened his own death. He was calculating, but the account was false. It was a costly building without foundation. And the satisfaction turns to terror.

But it is *life and peace to set the mind on the Spirit*. If we set the mind on the Spirit we do not seek our own spirit, for our own spirit already tells us that we are limited and that God alone can help us to transcend these limits by sending his Divine Spirit to man and meeting us on the way. God's meeting with us is grace. To define the essence of grace in relation to setting the mind on the Spirit would mean to allow grace to flow from the Spirit; to know that it comes from God but marks the way the Son went: coming from the Father and returning to the Father. Grace also forms a circle, but one of life, not of death. Not a circle that man laboriously constructs in the flesh and for the flesh, but a divine circle; sharing in the circulation of love in God. This is life and peace. Life because God is eternal, peace because God alone gives peace. Man is invited to share in this circulation of grace through God's Spirit. He bends before God in adoration and recognizes the Holy Spirit as his guide. This lays the foundation that guarantees eternal life, and the Son himself has paid the price for it.

Through the visibility of the Spirit and the efficacy of peace and the desire for eternal life man experiences a joyous relationship with God and his Spirit, which makes God the center. One now tries to move toward him and give himself to him. Because God is henceforth the center, an eternal center, man has no further need of worrying about his ego, his flesh, his concupiscence, which does not mean that he ceases to be a human being. He remains the Father's creature, redeemed by the Son. And he remains in the knowledge of the Son made flesh, who brought the Spirit into the world. Flesh is turned into an offering, is sacrificed. The flesh is no longer the center because something that has been sacrificed cannot be the center. When Abraham is ready to give up his son, neither he nor Isaac remains the center, only God alone. And when the Son obtains the Father's permission for his mission, he makes the Father the center. He shows in his life and his Cross what the Father shows in the Resurrection of the Son: that divine love is the center, that life and peace are victorious over everything, even the flesh.

7. *For the mind that is set on the flesh is hostile to God; it does not submit to God's law, indeed it cannot.*

The Incarnate Son shows us in his flesh how a man

can be open toward the Father, constantly submitted to his will, living by his love, in an enduring friendship with God that means an abiding presence, a seeking of the Father's will and joy in fulfilling it. Exchange of love, but also realization of it; creative, enduring, surrendered. The Son entirely makes the Father his center; he never questions the Father-Son relationship, but affirms it constantly and lives it clearly in all its meanings. *The mind that is set on the flesh is hostile to God*, turned away from God, rejects God; for man cannot possibly turn his gaze at the same time on himself and on God. He has to choose. If he chooses the flesh, God disappears from view. Man no longer looks in his direction. This is true not only regarding the explicit conscious relations he has with God, in prayer for example, which is now replaced by hostile silence. It is true for everything to do with God. For God's law also, since the flesh wants its own law and despises the law of God. Seeking its own, the flesh no longer recognizes the law of God. The new law brought by the Son is a law of community, of church, of enlargement of life and ever-renewed union with God; a law that invites, in which every word individually offers itself to man's participation, which is an opening, a beginning. The law of the flesh is closed in on itself and has nowhere an opening from which one could see the law of God. This lack of any window is the reason that the flesh *cannot* even recognize God's law. It is a thick wall. One who is committed to the flesh alone has forgotten to build openings; he has neglected the most elementary rules of architecture, because he was occupied solely with himself. In his thinking he missed out on what others had already recognized and what has become a general human experience.

When Paul knows and states so clearly how everything looks in the flesh and how it ought to look in the spirit, he does so not just for his own time but for every age. He offers a timeless vision because the new law is timeless and will never lose its newness in this or in any other respect. Man in a certain sense remains the same. The man of the flesh, then as today, is delivered over to the same experience of death, and the man of the spirit exposed to the breath of the same living Spirit. He will know the same life, the same peace. This teaches us something about the universal knowledge of God. He created every human being with the same nature, is related to each as Creator, and yet each one is different and unique because he forms a new relationship with each one and opens up for him a new possibility of love and of spirit in an infinite variety. Certain elements remain the same, but that which is not merely element but supernatural, coming from God as grace, can be infinitely different, an overflowing life in which there is no room for any kind of death.

8. *And those who are in the flesh cannot please God.*

Since God gave a body to man at creation, he gave him a form, a space, a boundary. But beside man he placed himself, the Infinite, and maintained immediate relations with man's spirit. Nothing was lacking to man; God made known to him what he needed to know. As long as he was without sin he could live in the Spirit of God, in the perfect spontaneity of his primitive existence. When man sinned, the boundaries appeared. When man breaks off the relationship with God, he needs to have an exact knowledge of his own boundary. He tries one thing or another, goes as far as he can, and each time experiences his limits. What man is, within his No to God, cannot give him ultimate satisfaction. So he tries to exalt the flesh beyond its own limits and make a god of it. Every step he takes in order to live more in the flesh renders his vision of God more dim. While he tries to break the bonds that bind him to God, God appears to him as some strange projection of his own fantasy, having nothing to say to him and he having even less to say to God. But God does not remain silent.

He is displeased with man's doings in the flesh, with the accentuation of the boundaries that God in his love had drawn in such a way that they need not have become conscious to man because he was living in the divine company. In paradise the boundaries of creatureliness were set in the vast space of God's infinity, they could neither be experienced nor measured. God's radiance was so forceful, his nearness so important, that existence was pure happiness. And when the new law of the Son makes its appearance and he bears in his flesh the Father's condemnation, God can no longer endure anyone who wants to live in the flesh. For such a one reverses the new relationship and does the opposite of what God expects of him in his self-seeking and desire for pleasure. The offer of grace to live in the spirit and find life and peace there is not only infinitely vast but also infinitely enduring. There is abundance for every moment. From this abundance man can live in the spirit. He has at his disposal all he needs; what he actually uses appears as quite minimal; it bears no comparison with the greatness of the offer.

9. But you are not in the flesh, you are in the Spirit, if the Spirit of God really dwells in you. Anyone who does not have the Spirit of Christ does not belong to him.

The division now passes through the believer. The Apostle takes it for granted that they are not in the flesh. This presupposes a rejection. A clear No, in the full Christian sense which is already there and creates the space for the Yes to the Spirit. Where the Spirit is there is no ambiguity. He brings the division that is at the same time discrimination. If we say Yes we know where our decision leads us, from what we separate ourselves, what the situation is that we create. Yes and No have as little to do with each other as life in the spirit has with life in the flesh. Neither is there the possibility of turning to one side at one time and to the other at another time, to say Yes just for the present, making a reservation about the future; or saying a loud Yes because the courage is lacking to say the No that is within.

There is the possibility of self-deception. We might think we have said Yes or No to certain aspects behind which lies the unknown, an adventure that we have not thought out. When the Spirit of Christ wholly lives in the believer, however, the assent is absolute. Turning to the Spirit we know it is not our own spirit we are seeking but the Spirit of the Lord, and we leave to him every space for Yes and No. Yes, that he may come to live in us; No, that he may continue to defend us; Yes again that the Spirit of the Lord may leave us no escape route and bolt the door against the sin of duplicity, of ambiguity. Our own spirit is weak, the Spirit of Christ is strong. Our own spirit is there and tries to take a step toward Christ—we could call it the step of merit—but we know that the whole way is taken over by Christ, who comes to meet us with his grace. The Spirit of the Lord is the Holy Spirit, who fulfills all conditions perfectly, who is impatient because he belongs to God and represents God; and he has also heard the assent of human weakness and makes himself responsible for it. He is concerned about keeping man within his assent and fills the weak Yes with divine strength. And the flesh needs to be forgotten. It will make itself felt, but will have to give way to the weight of the double Yes spoken by the spirit of man and the Spirit of Christ. The human spirit will also make itself felt and will try to win some rights back, or gain new ones; but the Spirit of *Christ* is watching, and not only at certain moments, for he *abides*. It is this quality that gives to our assent its actuality and its urgency. When we know the qualities of the Holy Spirit and know that they come from God the Spirit through God the Son into the creature made by God the Father, we realize that they can keep their place only through combat, and that fleshly man, who is inclined to fall away, does not tire of kicking against the goad.

10. But if Christ is in you, although your bodies are dead because of sin, your spirits are alive because of righteousness.

God's abiding in the believer brings about another separation. If God dwells in him change will take place. He has decided for the Lord, and now the Lord makes a new decision by his presence. These are two separate actions meeting in the contemplation of the Father, in his will and in his being. There is a special activity of Christ in the believer who has decided wholly for Christ; a communication of his mysteries hidden in the Triune life. The Incarnate God has lived and suffered in the hiddenness of the flesh on earth, in order to work once more in the same sense through the Divine Spirit in everyone who makes his decision for him, and places this choice anew into the hands of the Lord for his free disposal. He knows by a faith that not only hopes but is certain that the Lord *will* make a separation. The Lord separates in such a way that *your bodies are dead*, belong to death; the believer's rejection of the flesh receives in the death of the body a permanent ultimate expression *because of sin, but your spirits are alive because of righteousness* and justification.

The Son, who on the Cross is victorious over the death he first suffers, lets himself be raised from the dead by the Father. He celebrates his own Resurrection, but in total surrender to sinners, in total surrender to justification, to life. He does not want a life that is confined to himself or to God in his Triune Mystery. He wants the life of God within the life of men. The *Spirit* is entrusted with this task of life; he gives and maintains life; the spirit of the true believer is the spirit of the new teaching, Spirit of the Lord, Spirit of life. What might appear to his fellow men as his merely human spirit cannot be divided into Spirit of the Lord and spirit of the believer; the distinction between mine and yours no longer exists. Even in prayer and contemplation we cannot separate what is his and what belongs to the Holy Spirit (in order to join it again afterward). The Spirit takes over in him, works in him, transforms him, so that he is no longer aware of himself. Nor does he need such awareness because he is allowed to belong to the Lord in the same way as the Lord belongs to the Father, in an analogy that God alone can analyze. The believer does not need to analyze, this would even be a mistake because it could lead him to make some reservation in his surrender—or worse still, to measure the strength of his surrender.

The believer's spirit obeys now new directions and principles. These are not the law imposed by the limitations of human existence in space and time, for he has been reborn to life that is Christ, and he possesses

Christ. Life thus takes on at once the meaning and the fullness of the eternal. The infinite belongs to it. It is life proceeding from the mission of the Lord and into one's own Christian mission.

11. If the Spirit of him who raised Jesus from the dead dwells in you, he who raised Christ Jesus from the dead will give life to your mortal bodies also through his Spirit which dwells in you.

As Spirit of the Father, the Holy Spirit has raised up the Son in the Father's name. Here the unity between the Father and the Spirit becomes tangible. We touch here the Father's action through the Spirit in the Resurrection as closely as in the overshadowing of the Mother. The Spirit formed the Son's life in her. He carried the Father's seed as the expression of his will to her. And here again it is the Spirit of the Father as Holy Spirit in inseparable unity who acts in the Father's name: to bring life, to give back to the Father the living Son. The Son's body is fit for this resurrection; it belongs to the Father to such a degree that it answers the summons at once, in a readiness which is greater than that of Lazarus, because everything is done in God and through God. The Son's body is a body of purity and at the same time a spiritual body. But the same *Spirit who raised Jesus from the dead* will bring the bodies of all men to resurrection. These bodies know nothing of the readiness that answers the first summons, nor can they overcome death through any power of faith of

37

their own, but only because the Son was made flesh and possessed a body in which he bore the Father's condemnation and thus was victorious over death.

Because the human body through its belonging to the Son has become his dwelling, the Spirit can work in it as Spirit of the Father. Through him men receive the new life, through him who is superabundant life. No death can touch him who stood by the Son raising him up and who from now on stands by all who belong to the Son.

Thus a double connection can be traced: a connection of bodily life is created through the death and Resurrection of the Son. A connection of the spirit is created through the indwelling of the Father's Spirit in man. The Spirit cannot die, so he transforms his dwelling to make it share in eternal life. In principle the body is brought to submission in the believer through the life of the Spirit, the life of the Father, the life that the body of the Son shares with him. The mystical body, the eucharistic body, is no fiction. It is a reality that is stronger than our earthly ephemeral reality. A sick or elderly person, or one in critical condition, can from certain signs draw conclusions about the end of his days. He can almost calculate how much strength remains in his body. But he cannot calculate to what degree the life of the Lord in him is stronger than his approaching death, stronger even than his present life when he possessed it in its prime and fullness. And this life of the Lord, shared out among countless believers throughout the ages, suffers no diminishment in strength. Though it is the vital principle the Christian possesses through faith, it cannot be confined to a form. It is a presence of surpassing radiance and life. Of the senses and at the same time suprasensual. Of the senses, for the Christian can represent to himself what the Son has experienced, seen, tasted by making an image of the Son from what he has heard and himself experienced. This image is drawn, molded from and rooted in both the eternal being of the Lord and the imagination of man. Suprasensual, because ultimately he cannot form an image of the divine essence that is a reality transcending all life, supreme above all imagination. This suprasensuality reveals not only the ever-greater Lord but also the ever-greater God and the transcendence of eternal life itself. It becomes apparent that everything else was a preparation for a goal that lies so far in God that man will never reach it. He moves toward it, strives and seeks for it, but suddenly grace takes over and the moment of this transition he cannot describe.

The life of the Father's Spirit is not only super-abundantly alive in the believer but especially so in God himself. As Divine Spirit he beholds and accompanies the believer's bodily death and invents ecclesial means in the sacraments to give a Christian form to this death, to accompany it in a humanly visible way, to lead it through prayer into the world that is only prayer; and yet he cannot reveal himself in full visibility because his life is so strong, unique and extraordinary that the center, the kernel, the essential substance remains hidden in the Triune God. Something of it remains visible in the Son's revelation on earth, something in his word, something in the fulfillment of his promises, but all these traces together do not make the total. But the sum total is in the believer—communicated by God himself, who remains eternal life and gives it, in giving it, reveals that he does not cease to be the same eternal life.

II

THE INHERITANCE

*12. So then brethren, we are debtors, not to the flesh, to
live according to the flesh.*

Paul calls those who are his own "*brethren*". This
brotherhood has now a special meaning relating to
the Spirit. They are brethren because they live
according to the new law that not only obliges them
but binds them to each other. Each one responds to
the directions of the law as perceived by him not only
in solitude and isolation but in the community of the
brethren. In responsibility toward the brethren that
generates genuine brotherhood at the same time as it
allows them to find its true spirit. They have to listen
as brothers.

Now each of them has a body and knows the law of
the flesh. He has experienced what it means to be
flesh and to be subject to the flesh. But this meaning is
much more limited than they perhaps thought.

No permanent bond, no obligation arises from it.
They owe nothing to the flesh, especially not *to live
according to the flesh*. This can also be interpreted in
this way: the flesh is there, but it belongs to the
obligations imposed on the spirit. In every Christian

the spirit must be in control, so that the flesh appears only as a concomitant, something in which the genuineness of the spirit can be tested, an addition to the spirit conditioned by creation, condemned because of sin, judged by the Father in the flesh of the Son in order to hold its rightful place now in every believer. Renunciation does not mean annihilation. Renunciation is something new, fecund, liberating, offering new access to the Spirit. Perhaps it would appear more simple, since the flesh exists, to allow it its own law and submit to it, whatever kind of satisfaction or possession might be in question. But there is no law that could claim to be independent of the spirit. This freedom from the law, from obligation and debt to the flesh, adds something positive to the spirit: a superiority that strengthens the spirit, makes it immune and provides a guarantee that it is true spirit that is not nourished by the flesh but by the Spirit, the Holy Spirit. This is true for all the brethren. And the brotherhood is strengthened by the submission of each one of the brothers to this truth.

13. *For if you live according to the flesh you will die, but if by the Spirit you put to death the deeds of the body you will live.*

Body and death are linked, the germ of death is hidden in the flesh. Each time a man thinks of his death, he knows that he has moved nearer to it, that death, sown in him, has grown and become more present. A man who lives according to the flesh will submit to this law of the flesh and to the approach of the last hour. With the certainty of death in view, he will try to draw out of his flesh as much enjoyment and satisfaction as possible, perhaps with the despair of a criminal condemned to death who clings to the last joys, in resistance to everything that is not flesh and death.

And so death has far greater power because it includes everything that is flesh and law of the flesh. The connection between mortal body and the thought of death becomes more and more stringent. And so not only the thought of death, but even the hour of death will of necessity weigh more and more heavily on man. *You shall die* is changed into *I am mortal*, which becomes the ever-present truth marking all the deeds of man. Finally he has nothing left that is free from this relentless idea.

The deeds of the Spirit, life in the Spirit and acceptance of the new law, however, are opposed to death. The Spirit is not something vague that accompanies man on his road and to which he would be able to reach out in certain hours in order to seek help and support. The Spirit is possession and center, Holy Spirit, living in man and infusing deeds of the Spirit into him, so that in the strength of God man can do the works of God. Such is the Father's gift to men at the moment when he endows his Son with a body. For God himself responds to his gift by giving to man the gift of his Spirit, who has the capacity of working divinely no less than the Son as man has gained the capacity of working humanly.

From now on man can do things that are in opposition and superior to the deeds of the flesh. The Spirit silences the flesh. The Spirit has the power of preventing the deeds of the flesh, either by destroying their consequences or by paralyzing them in action, or else by rejecting them from the outset as unimportant and devoid of good. In this opposition of the Spirit it becomes evident that he is life; the life by which the faithful live, and exactly at the point where death should begin. It is victory of life over death, like the victory of the Resurrection over death. In the Cross the deeds of our sinful bodies have been atoned for, extinguished in such a way that we cannot understand how it comes to pass; we cannot understand or imitate the work of the Cross, but can only accept it humbly in faith and experience it in its effects. Something similar happens in the life we have to live when we put to death the deeds of the flesh through the Spirit. Death has changed its position; it is no longer in us but outside of us. It does not strike us, it is struck by us. Activity and passivity have exchanged their meaning. The whole relationship of the created world to God appears totally transformed through his giving us his life; it is no longer an individualistic life (over which sin can reign) but a life of brothers who have been redeemed through the Spirit and called together to life.

14. For all who are led by the Spirit of God are sons of God.

If a believer wants to form an idea of life, he is conscious that he will not find it in his fellow men, but only in God and above all in the Holy Spirit. He sees the works of the Spirit: they reveal divine life, the strength of God's power. To see them means growth of Christian faith. All the tendencies stirring toward life in the Christian, toward life in God, are made to bear fruit. The Spirit leads; he urges forward so mightily that the one thus driven is delivered over to him in faith, in order henceforth not to be driven by anyone else. He learns from the Spirit to forget what is his own and live in the divine. He is like one subjected, a mercenary in the service of the Spirit. The Spirit blows wherever he pleases, and the one led by the Spirit has to hand himself over to the Spirit to be blown wherever the Spirit wishes. He does not himself perceive the plans and intentions of the Spirit. He can only allow things to happen. Every new animation by the Spirit begets new life, guaranteed by life itself, which is the Spirit. If a believer has a mission, it can happen that God shows him tasks that are to be done and goals to be reached, and then through the Spirit he demands other things from the one who obeys that seem to be hardly compatible with what went before, as if the direction were changed, pointing elsewhere. But the one who prays feels under obedience in whatever case: in receiving the mission, in carrying it out and in the apparent eclipse of the mission. For the Father in the Spirit brings the missions of the faithful into conformity with that of the Son; he does not want to make their way too easy by revealing the goal or the hour beforehand.

On account of this conformity he regards those he commissions as sons. This regard of God is efficacious; they really become sons in the all-embracing obedience of the Son. And the Spirit drives and blows and brings forth all that is called life in the believer, and there is no distance from God nor is there a disposition in man that is not included within this blowing of the Spirit. Whether the nearness is felt less immediately, whether difficulties accumulate, God remains near. He never separates himself from the Spirit as long as he lives in the believer. He remains present and recognizable in all the leadings. The sonship to the Father rests on the leading of the Spirit. It is sonship within the mission of the Son and his movement: coming from God and returning to God, as is characteristic for the Son. The same Spirit who led the Son of God leads sinners also into an ever-deeper and larger faith and makes them achieve in his power all the things the Father expects from them and in which he wants to recognize the mark of the Son and so of sonship. Loneliness, doubt, disgust, weariness, powerlessness, suffering: all this is included in the leading of the Spirit and serves the one so led as a road sign so to say, where he can read that all is well, that he is becoming a son at a distance from Christ, but in his love fully experienced.

*15. For you did not receive the spirit of slavery to fall
back into fear, but you have received the spirit of sonship.
When we cry out "Abba! Father!" . . .*

The spirit of slavery creates a fixed distance; it is not
possible to bridge it over, for slavery binds the spirit
to an inferior place to which it is strictly confined. In
a graphic representation man would stand as a small
point at the bottom, immovable, once and forever. It
is there he would have to live. Neither prayer nor
sacrifice nor knowledge through the spirit (which
would be a *spirit of slavery*) would have power to
enlarge this space and shorten the distance to God, to
make room for grace or procure for man a free and
dynamic access to God whom he adores. The boast of
the slave would be to have been nothing else but a
slave at every stage of his life. He would, though
grateful, strictly reject approaches, tokens of affec-
tion, favors from his lord, so that no encroachment
occurs, and he could never pride himself on having
learned anything intimate about his master or having
been favored with a higher rank.

All this would militate against the honor of his state
in life. He would have to fear not only having defined
his place too narrowly but equally having over-
reached his due. Both excesses would arouse the
anger and revenge of his master, so that fear and
slavery are inseparably united. Through his state, his
place as servant, man would be condemned to *fall*

47

back into fear again. The life of the Old Covenant would return in which the sinner had only one option, which is to be a slave. But God sent his Son into the world, and to be Son is his innermost quality. In this quality as Son, he has taken out of love the place of the slave and as such has taken on himself and fulfilled the task his Father has set him and which the sin of the world demanded. But by becoming slave without ceasing to be Son, he also represented and sacrificed what was ours before his coming. He has bestowed nobility on the state of slavery, the whole human state that he held for thirty-three years. Recruited by the Son for the same state, we can now become with him sons, chosen and adopted sons. The Spirit of the Father is so infinite that he can accept and recognize us also in the Son's place. This recognition however, which is a gift, demands a response from us. We should be quite sure of this. We must not hanker for our old place and stubbornly live in fear. Our response is to cry out together with Christ: *Abba! Father!* The response is recognition; it is also obligation, it is responsibility, faith. Faith within love, in the new hope given by the state of sonship. Were we to draw another representation of our relationship with God, the place of man would no longer be a point at the bottom, but all over the chart; he would be able to fulfill his place everywhere in the way God wants it, without fear of failure.

16.   . . . It is the Spirit himself bearing witness with our spirit that we are children of God.

The Spirit of God is witness and testimony. By witnessing to our spirit he lifts it to a higher level and enables it to receive the testimony, to understand it. The Spirit confirms therefore that we are children of God; but he does not confirm it within a sphere of God to which we have no access, but to our spirit. He accepts therefore that our spirit exists and is capable of understanding his witness. For us this means that we know about this capacity, that we take part in this witness of which the highest content is: we are *children of God.* The mystery is revealed. We are no longer waiting in the place of slavery for unclear and uncertain things. We are children to whom the Father reveals himself, and our spirit receives the fullness of the message. And in this acceptance of the message a totally new light is thrown on this testimony that is the whole life and sacrifice of the Son. We do not make the mistake of putting ourselves in the place of the Son; we have not suddenly become gods, heavenly beings, unfit for the tasks of this earth. Such as we were we have been received into the new truth and teaching, into a place to which we were destined beforehand by the Father who wanted to make us his adopted children. If we are believers and our spirit hears the message of the Spirit, then we cannot complain of not knowing where our faith is directed, what we shall do with our hope or where our reward is. The whole plan of God is revealed before our eyes, and we can say a valid Yes to the Spirit who explains it to our spirit. This consent has quite a different form from the consent given by the Lord's Mother to the angel. For her it was made harder; she only knew the Son from the promise, and she carried him all alone. Our consent takes place within the fulfillment and in the community. Led by Paul we are allowed to cry out *Abba Father* together, in the certainty given by the Spirit that we call God by the right name, for we are truly his children.

17. If children, then heirs, heirs of God and fellow heirs with Christ, provided we suffer with him in order that we may also be glorified with him.

To be child is to be heir, that is the law of life and above all the law of the new teaching: in love. Within this childhood there is no exclusion. To be child of the Father means to be joined to the eternal Son with the right of the same things he has a right to.

This interconnection is at first hidden away in the love of where the new teaching has its foundation: in the exchange of love in the Trinity. But through the witness of the Spirit they are made known to those who believe, not in order to cradle them in a false security, exempting them from an effort of their own, but so that they may grasp the greatness of their faith and of the gift of life. If the Old Testament left many questions open regarding the relationship of the believer to God and regarding his intentions, the fulfillment of the New Testament has an answer of love for every question even before it is asked. This total answer was first given by the Father to the Son, as a gift he brought down to earth. He knew how his life would develop on earth, he knew about his return. And when the Passion temporarily covered everything with darkness, so much that he cried out: "My God, my God, why have you forsaken me?", during this darkest hour the certainty of the heritage was laid up within his sonship, ready to be communicated to men, not as a merely external addition to their faith, but rather as its foundation.

Paul speaks to Christians—but Christians also can hesitate because they do not understand sufficiently what happened to them when they accepted the faith. The Apostle therefore wants them to look anew at this relationship to God, not in an abstract way, but in the reality of the Incarnate God: they should learn to look at their inheritance in the same way as Christ himself looks at it. They should see eternal life in this inheritance, the fullness of which no one can imagine, because it is the fullness of the Triune God and of all the inhabitants of Heaven and of each individual among them. Fullness of love, fullness of faith and hope; and in the hope that has been promised to faith and in the fulfillment of hope taken possession of in Heaven. The inheritance is the Father's eternity, he possesses and creates it. It is the eternity of the Son who for a moment becomes visible as separated from this heavenly possession in his pure sonship so that his right to it may become visible, that the human laws as they are known to men may be applied to him, and it may become more clear that everything that belongs to the Father in Heaven belongs also to the Son. There is a juridical relationship of inheritance that man knows from his everyday life; he also knows how it feels to hope for an inheritance and to look forward to it. A son lives in his father's house that he will inherit one day, with his steps he measures the father's fields that will become his; he resolves to take them over and administer them in his father's spirit. He knows this spirit and the tradition of the farm or family. And if the believer now may feel himself to be fellow heir with the Divine Son who perfectly fulfills the paternal law, he knows all of a sudden with a new responsibility that he must receive the Spirit of the Father in such a way as to have it in himself and pass it on. His faith becomes a "remaining in the Spirit"; he has grown into the responsibility of the house of God; he has accepted the burden of the inheritance. There is one way to realize this Spirit: the way of the Son, *provided we suffer with him*.

This is now taken for granted, there is readiness, obedience, attention to everything that concerns the Son; this is not indiscreet, no pushing of oneself, it is simply justified fellowship. The sharing in everything that belongs to the Son, in his sufferings also, leads in itself further, *so that we may also be glorified with him*. Both are so close together that the transition appears abrupt, even incomprehensible. But as soon as the body of Christ and its inheritance stand before the eyes of faith, no contradiction exists any longer; it balances itself in the one way. In the one absolute total surrender which does not ask but in a few words points out the direction that the Son took, while all things were made for him and now suddenly appear as additions to his sufferings and glorification. The last addition is man himself: man in obedience, entitled to obey. This right belongs to the privileges of the heir.

18.   I consider that the sufferings of this present time are not worth comparing with the glory that is to be revealed in us.

The sufferings of this present time are, for Christians, present sufferings in the light of the sufferings of the Lord. The Son did not want to know the Hour, only the certainty of its coming. For the believer there is a double sharing in possible suffering. The first because of sin, where suffering is punishment, at best reparation. And probably no day passes without our being reminded of the existence of such suffering in one form or another and our having to bear our part. The other sharing is the knowledge of the Lord's suffering, a knowledge that stretches from knowledge of the sins of all humanity in which I have my share, to knowledge and experience of the death of the Lord, who died for all sins and all sinners. Faith invites our sharing. It invites our prayer and meditation, our acceptance of sacrifices that we offer to the Lord in order to prove our willingness to be present with him. There is also suffering that is imposed and has the character of the here and now because the sufferer does not want to leave the Lord and accepts from his hand whatever is given him, which is above all a grace and a joy, but also at once points to the Cross, to loneliness and death. And in the same way as the Lord suffered until the last moment and did not leave a drop behind in the chalice, so we are, as long as we live, capable of suffering, though to a much lesser degree. No one may accept only the joy of life and reject all real experience of suffering in body or spirit. Suffering is our entry into participation, and participation in the Lord's suffering fundamentally knows no measure. No one can say: so far only; more would be exaggerated, less would be imperfect. The measure is never in our hands. All measure is still more withdrawn on the Cross. But whatever be the sum of suffering, Paul is convinced *that the sufferings of this present time are not worth comparing with the glory* that is to come. That is the foundation of Christian hope, which points to what is to come that can only be glorious because it takes place in eternal life and because *what is to be revealed in us* are things that would not be revealed without us.

We must be there. We may even say: if Christ in a certain sense needs our suffering as participation, as a sign that we have said Yes and that his redemption is effective in us, he needs us in a much more important sense in Heaven, in order to reveal his glory in us. It will be in us that what makes the divine principle, which is love, fully resplendent takes place. In us: we will be the objects, and we shall experience this love as subjects, as children of God and fellow heirs with Christ. It will be the experience of every individual and the experience of the Church triumphant, in communion with the Lord, but also with all those present in love. Present in love, because God places them there, but also because God's indwelling is fulfilled afresh in Heaven and is no longer experienced in a hidden way as a beginning, but openly and fully realized. This experience will be most highly personal and at the same time most universally catholic: each will experience the glory of God in God and in each neighbor and in himself; he will enjoy and communicate it. And so the last meaning of this receiving of glory will be revealed: receiving in order to give, as the Son accepted his human life in order to give it back to the Father on the Cross, to be raised by him from the dead, to enter anew into his glory. Love is circulation of giving and receiving, whose dimension now grows to the dimension of the divine exchange of love, surpassing not only our understanding but also our faith. We can only get hold of it in small pieces in our faith on earth, which reveal almost nothing of the whole mosaic to us.

If glory is announced so quickly after the announcement of our being fellow heirs, then we must learn from this that Heaven and its full life for us is like a treasure that we can only guess at here below.

We have a certain interest in it, but this is only fully awakened when we receive the treasure and can dispose of it at will, where it is *to be revealed in us*. It is not a question of a miser's selfish joy in glittering jewels hidden away, but of joy in the splendor seen in the hands of others, in all the improbable expressions possible to the love whose immeasurable value God now reveals in us.

III

THE HOPE

19. For creation waits with eager longing for the revealing of the sons of God.

God has created all things for the Son. This end for which they exist means enablement to share much that is beyond them and which yet lives with them a life God infuses into them. There is in the world an undefined yearning that was unknown to Adam and about which he could say nothing because it appears only gradually after the Fall as an accompaniment, a quest for something quite different; and the quest already seems out of all proportion, for the first sin is incalculable and the sinner knows no answer to it. Time on earth gives no answer either. To be created for the Son is in accord with an intention of the Triune God. But this does not mean anything as yet to the world, except that it becomes gradually conscious of this direction: there will come a possibility of return sometime. Also, that the world is the answer to a call from the Son, to a need, a will, a right to what has been created for him.

Man, becoming conscious of his being created in the midst of all other creatures of the Father, knows of two relationships (quite distinct from the fact of being created): a relationship with all other creatures of whom the Creator made him Lord. He sees the ascending line in nature, the hierarchy and himself in the first place. Nothing that has been created surpasses him in value. From this a responsibility accrues to him, a shared destiny that points to an origin in God and to a divine plan. His mere existence, however, is not the goal; there is a providence that is shaping a future destiny for him, is taking him somewhere. In this he experiences for the first time a vague intimation of his being created for the Son. This double relationship changes its character in the course of the Old Covenant. In the promises the direction toward the Son becomes clearer, but in the growing distance from God the first phase also, the rule over all creatures, receives clearer contours. These two directions could serve to provide a balance for man within his movement and could clarify his own place. But as soon as he refuses to obey God and remain within the law, turning his face away, his place appears to him more unsure and uncertain; he cannot define it himself though he knows that he is incapable of changing his place or even making it appear irrelevant. It becomes ever clearer that man's being created for something other is a fact inherent in the whole of creation. The whole world is full of longing.

The creation, says the Apostle, indicates a community. All created things are held together not only through a hierarchical order with man at the top or through a glance backward to the common origin but through something quite different that binds creation together in a new way, makes it a unity in something that is for the time being an eager longing for a revelation, taking hold of man too, the longing for a new definition of and light on the meaning of all things. In his creaturehood and in the first words addressed to man by the Father there was already a kind of revelation, but it was soon covered over, lost again, laid up somewhere where man cannot reach it. He cannot identify his own place with that of revelation. And now the place of revelation is defined anew; the promises, the coming of the Son show this place; the place of the Triune God, Heaven, eternity, God's infinity. All revelation comes from there. But that is not all. When men become participators through faith in the sonship of the Son of God and fellow heirs in Heaven with the one who appeared on earth, they also receive the revelation. Children of God reveal together with the Son of Man what the Son of Man alone is both able to reveal and has revealed; through his Cross and Resurrection he now wants to reveal it together with his brothers.

If we had no tradition it would be possible for someone who does not know the Church and is suddenly confronted with the word of Sacred Scripture to see no more in it than a fascinating historical document, but one which would mean nothing to him in his present personal situation: he would only learn that there once was a man who called himself the Son of God and talked about matters which meant something at the time as fulfillment of prophecies and which appealed to his disciples, leading them to be his followers. But the word of Scripture has a revelatory meaning here and now—Church and tradition are founded on this and firmly built on this. For God offers to his own ever-new possibilities of revelation that are all contained in his Word, but he counts on man being able to show the whole meaning of his revelation. He already counted on man when he presented the sinful human form in utter purity, by declaring man's body, his fleshly garment, his own. That was his *kenosis*. But he also opened to man a new place on the heights, his own; he worked miracles for man, fed the crowd with a few loaves and fishes, raised Lazarus from the dead and showed in this way what man really is, his hidden truth; he made unglamorous man very special, he gave him so much of his light that he became a light himself. Light of his light, but only in analogy to the way in which the Son himself is light of the Father. He showed it with greatest radiance in his saints who are men among men and are suddenly able to work miracles in his name and see and reveal depths in his Word that until then had not been understood and had remained obscure. His own light was so powerful that it constantly lit new sources of light; his humanity was so deeply rooted on earth that new possibilities of revelation were given to men; his teaching was so powerful that it is always new, today and tomorrow and in a hundred years. Taken individually, out of his context, a saint would no longer be a saint; he who lives by God's Word would become as one who is himself famished. Only united to him are the revealers a revelation. They do no more than what God places within them, what they can show forth in the light given by God, as mediators of his revelation-mediators to whom the light was mediated; draftsmen who are themselves a drawing; artists who are a painting, just as God created man in his image, and the Son took this image and infused new features into it from the original. Because the children of God take part in the revelation of the Son, and the world, though redeemed, is still crying for redemption, it is filled with anxious longing, with a burning expectation, with one unique question that demands the unique answer.

Nature has a right to shine in the full light of God, the tree has a right to be a tree as God meant it to be; all the light of which nature has been robbed by sin must be poured over it. The seed dies, nature dies away; but in its death there lies a waiting, it is being made ready for the reception of the new revelation.

20.   For creation was subjected to futility, not of its own will but by the will of him who subjected it in hope.

Again all created things appear as a unity, but no longer in unity before the Creator, the unity of concord, but in the unity of futility, of vanity, giving

61

the impression of a foreign power robbing and devouring and consuming all that has been brought forth. Creation is not in agreement with this, it does not choose this fate of its own volition, this has been forced on it. It is a consequence of sin. No longer did the Creator have sole power over the world, nor did sin by itself have power through the individual sinner, but all sin together as a power in nature, as vanity and futility. A power that reveals itself and that causes things to happen that no one likes. It is not a foreign power, because it was called, provoked by sin, and its extent becomes apparent through sin. This power exerts itself. It does not subject the individual but the whole. When all things came into being and Adam ruled over animals and plants, he was given power that certainly could not be compared with the Creator's power but was sufficient and proportioned to man according to the plan of God. But Adam was not content with this power, and through his first sin he unleashed powers that once released took effect not only in the individual but in the whole. It was like a counterimage of revelation, which is to become visible through one man in the whole. Thus in one man the power of evil showed itself—not as if he himself had done all the evil personally, but through the choice of one evil he opened the way for more evil. And so evil subjects the world to vanity that expands and shows itself in everything.

Every new manifestation of it calls for even more

visibility, new forms of visibility. It is a form containing all forms in itself, an evil capable itself of every evil; something that was hidden has now become visible and overruns every limit to visibility. The whole creation appears in these words of the Apostle like a ball rolling into the abyss; quite different plans had been made for it, but now it falls out of the player's hands and becomes subject to alien laws. Everyone who looks at these words can see in them the mirrored image of what takes place in himself. No one ever chooses futility, but the world has become a thing of futility, and everyone knows how futile and full of vanity he is himself. If he knew it fully he would set himself against it; but he has only a half-knowledge of it, only by comparing himself with others and in playing together with others in a way that is in itself futility. He cannot separate his own vanity from that of others, so he prefers not to look at it and not to consider seriously that he, like the rest of the world, has been handed over to futility. This having been handed over occurred not according to his own choice and will; it fell upon him. It appears as the freedom of evil to which all gates stand open once one gate has been opened. The freedom of the children of God is shown in Adam until the fall into sin. It is shown anew in the Son of Man in whom it is a freedom of pure love, which has chosen obedience. Obedience and futility exclude each other.

21. Because creation itself will be set free from its bondage to decay and obtain the glorious liberty of the children of God.

A reckoning not yet completed: that is God's confrontation with the devil. It would be completed, if it were not for creation standing between them with all its swaying and wavering, its uncertainties and wrong decisions, its sin. But as it exists, God has to respect it. He gave it freedom, freedom of decision, freedom to choose with the consequent suffering. Everything is constantly offered anew, man is always free to decide and choose again; he can even, from the place he has chosen again for himself, make a new choice, because once and for all there is hope, hope added to everything else. Hope already in time that is passing away, hope reaching to knowledge, hope of the whole world toward Heaven, hope as a concomitant of the fact that all things are created for the Son. In the midst of vanity there is hope for redemption.

Man is conscious of his slavery and that all things share in it and of the fact that mortality and decay are signs of slavery. However, the punishment God has decreed for man is neither unlimited nor final; it is in no wise absolute, because the signs of living hope are to be found everywhere. This hope is a ray of divine light, a permanent opening in the closing door, a tomorrow in the midst of a today that already seems to belong to yesterday. Hope is hope of liberation, and that means of the possibility of a new choice that would lead men to become children of the glory of God. The whole of mankind, from the most hardened sinner to the true coheir with Christ, possesses this hope, small perhaps, dull and hardly visible, yet hope that is irresistible. God leaves no creature without it. Everywhere he makes it enter, so that a spark of his word, his will and his planning, of his omnipresence, should be everywhere present. And in the same way as a captive in his prison is waiting for some miracle to come all of a sudden and bring freedom and light and life, so every man in his captivity on earth is hoping for something powerful that will burst open his present condition and make him heir in freedom and love. In every No that he utters, in every finality he chooses, he has to experience faintly the Yes and the promise of something quite different. The absolute belongs so fully to God that man can seek it only there. The way that leads there is signaled by hope that continues to exist in the midst of all this vanity. Hope shimmers at all times as a light of grace from God, bending over men as an unfathomable freedom not yet understood. If the captive thinks of freedom, it is of something he has not got but which he could have, and he paints it for himself with the brightest and most promising colors.

What the Christian paints for himself is of still greater promise, for it reaches to where the painting ends in order to make way for the reality of God and its own outline and, finally, vision. The one who sees is free, and time and space belong to him. Since the

Father has given creation to man to rule over, man can never be envisioned apart from it. Creation is part of him, and God has never taken back his gift. It is part not only of the believer but of every man. Man can distort, darken and discolor it, but he can also make it part of his hope and his faith. Then it participates in the light that falls on him. He cannot take hold of anything for himself alone that is not equally meant for everything created. Even in the deepest solitude he cannot think of himself as being so exclusive as to have the promise of salvation for himself while perdition is threatening the created world. Plants and animals belong to the sphere of his life, the wide earth, the intimacy of a home, the familiarity of a landscape. He cannot separate himself from it even when he is a captive. The world shares his destiny. If he is imprisoned, so is the world. When he, a captive, calls for liberation, he paints it in the images of the created world that has become inaccessible to him and is thus more than ever companion of his captivity and loneliness, thus accentuating his aloneness even more. And as the whole of creation shares in the vanity, it also shares in the hope. And hope means for creation in all its beauty and wildness, in its captivity, its dream of freedom, access to the Creator, to his presence and his love. God showed the same love on the first day of creation that he showed on the Sabbath-day; he said: "It is very good" to everything: the fishes and birds, the animals and man.

*22. We know that the whole creation has been groaning
in travail together until now.*

When Paul here uses the word *now*, he means a Now
that never ends, even when the echo of the word has
died away. He means a state that has been touched by
redemption but is on the point of changing or being
able to change into a real state of redemption. Precise
individual points of time, such as creation, or the
death of the Son on the Cross, are decisive points in a
history which is ever in progression and in which the
Now expresses a capacity to receive, to be made
fruitful, to change and to grow. Until now everything created has suffered. The Lord has redeemed
the world, but the world takes no notice of its
redemption. There is a power of resistance in it that it
does not want to lose. This unwillingness is a direct
consequence of sin, and the world's sorrow is part of
it, a suffering in solidarity with all creation, groaning
under the sin of mankind. This suffering has become
a permanent state. It knows acute forms, but also dull
persistence, and this in consequence of a resignation
that knows nothing better but simply remains in its
rut; it is perhaps even a form of consent to the suffering. Not consent to the Cross and to redemption;
not informed by hope in a complete transformation
in the sense that hope would give a meaning to the
will to suffer. It is consent for lack of insight because
it knows only itself.

But the world is a unity in the eyes of God, creatures have been created in rank and order; nothing has become disconnected or has been left to itself without participation, without fellow creatures. Everything created had its place in the world, and the world was a whole. This concept of a whole is inscribed in everything that has been created and accepted by it as something alive and active. There is togetherness, companionship, solidarity that is not only obvious to the eye but reaches much more deeply because this interconnection points to the Creator. This solidarity of created things is found not only in what they are but also in what they do: the capacity to suffer and the ability to hope belong to this. The whole of creation therefore shares in the great suffering Adam inflicted on God. It is torn along into the fate of man. Since it was made subject to man it has the capacity of sharing his suffering.

The world is a world full of pain—*until now*. And this Now penetrates everything in spite of all breakthroughs and interruptions, in spite of the fact that it can also contain joy and gratitude and love, in spite of the fact that individuals at the time of Paul had already become perfectly converted to God in a genuine following of the Son; that Stephen had suffered martyrdom and had seen Heaven open in the joy of his mission fulfilled. And though the Lord has risen from the dead and ascended to Heaven, the world *until now* has remained a world full of suffering. The *until now* is linked to passing time, and time has not yet passed away. There are irruptions of eternity into time, of eternal joy into the passing, but until now, enduring suffering. And in the midst of it all, since the world remains linked together by this very suffering, there is the hope of which the Apostle speaks and which cannot be conquered by all the continuing suffering.

23.   And not only creation, but we ourselves, who have the first fruits of the Spirit, groan inwardly as we wait for adoption as sons, the redemption of our bodies.

Suffering linking creation as a unity does not stop short before man. Man also suffers. He suffers and groans because he has to *wait*. This waiting that has been transformed by Christian hope appeared in some way unbearable before the coming of Our Lord, conditioned by the passing of time and the decay of all things. Before the Fall Adam did not know this kind of waiting. When God walked in paradise it was in a present now for Adam also. He did not have to wait for that moment, in longing and calculation; every moment of whatever event brought its fullness. Now in the Christian life hope has transformed the waiting, but without wholly taking away its character of painful longing. Man suffers. He suffers because the promises made to him have not yet all been fulfilled for him. He knows about his *adoption as son* by God, but it has not been visibly accomplished. He hopes. But his hope is not final certainty. If it were, the consequences of sin, suffering, punishment and reparation would be effaced.

And as ardently as he hopes for sonship, he also

hopes for the *redemption of his body*, which is burden-some to him and has innumerable possibilities of suffering and therefore is ever a warning to him. And this groaning in expectation, which unites him with everything that is created, is also meant to reconcile him in Christian faith with the Lord's Passion, giving him a participation in it. God has redeemed the world, but the process of redemption is in need of man; in him it needs that which links him to the Son's Cross: suffering, pain and groaning. Hope does not want to cover up the road the Son has trod, but to reveal it in order to give participation in it. Man's body and spirit are capable of participation. And even and especially those *who have the first fruits of the Spirit* and have understood his message, who have allowed him to live and work in themselves in such a way as to be made mindful of the suffering in order to build a kind of bridge to the sufferings of the Lord: in them the Holy Spirit sharpens the sense of solidarity not only with the Triune God and the Redeemer, but also with every sinner. In order to become free, the Christian is bound anew to both sides: to Heaven and to the world.

24. *For in this hope we were saved. Now hope that is seen is not hope. For who hopes for what he sees?*

Wherever in the Old Testament the promises are mentioned, the image is lacking. There are words for a time to come, but these words have, so to say, no connecting links, they do not form sentences. They belong so much to a world that is in God, and to a future world, that the image remains completely veiled. Even the temptation to form an image of redemption hardly exists. The difficulties are too great, the content of the words is too transcendent, the whole seems to burst the framework of faith. But statements continue to be made; the prophets speak words that have a meaning; the content of their words is attractive to those who hear them. But as soon as one tries to take hold of them more clearly, they dissolve. Other people and their sin, our own sin, the burden of the law and its opaqueness, do not urge us to a faith that can result in insight. The distance has become too great. And there are also the many threatening words of God, there is the mortality and decay of our own flesh, our aging and suffering. The picture man has of his earthly existence is so well arranged and fortified against words from without, that it would almost be expecting too much to demand its surrender in order to make room for something new; or that the little stones of the mosaic be kept so loose that room remains for the promise, or even for the fulfillment that will explode everything.

In the New Covenant when God became man and proclaimed his teaching, when the impossible suddenly became possible—God is close, he is among us, he forgives our trespasses, he gives us the sacramental life that is always explosive—in the New Covenant God brings the image with him. But in it there is something that is revealed and something that remains hidden. What is revealed is the perfection in God, the fullness of grace in his Word, and the fullness in those who are his own, who work miracles in his name and break the bread. The old order is breaking up, hope is triumphing over everything. It is no longer hope in the fulfillment of a promise, for the promise is fulfilled. But there is a superabundance of fullness that contains the immensity of what has not been revealed. Hope was lived in love by the Lord in such a way that it becomes a part of faith: the visible part. But in the visible the invisible is contained, in the image the unimaginable. God does not show us something and then withdraw it again; but he calls, and within the answer hope will be fulfilled whenever it may be, without an image of it having been given beforehand. The image is in God. It is no longer in us, as it was in the Old Testament. The fact that it lies in God means that it is hidden. It is the uninterrupted intimacy of the Triune God, who from the vastness of his love will fulfill everything man hopes for. And the hour belongs to God.

As the Son did not know the hour of the Passion, so the hour of the fulfillment of hope will come without our knowing it beforehand. Everything we learn through the new teaching and every response we give confirms our hope but does not show the fulfillment. It is necessary for the fulfillment of hope that a large amount of faith be expended. Man has to live in faith so that hope will remain, but God's love will fulfill everything at the hour chosen by God. There is therefore no to and fro in hope, no advancing forward in order to be thrown back again, because hope entire rests in God, and the way to it is a faith entire; the goal lies in the entire Word of God and its ultimate comprehension. Everything we experience as Christians, everything we attempt to do in love, every prayer and every expression of faith increases hope. But only in and through God will this increase reach its final fullness. Yet hope is an essential part of faith. We cannot believe and refuse to hope. We cannot walk in love and not desire the goal. But we must have the courage to strive for a goal that is still covered up. Everything we can grasp, what we receive, what God allows to reach us from the self-giving of the Cross through whatever channels of his grace, belongs to the fulfillment, not to hope. The content of hope, even if it can be circumscribed with words of faith, remains hidden and is inaccessible to us. And it belongs again to faith that we leave an open space for this superabundance in every fulfillment, and therefore for hope.

25. And hoping for what we cannot see means awaiting it with patient endurance.

What we hope for is not visible, but nonetheless we have to remain open and alert in its regard: this means, not one way today and another tomorrow, but to persevere with constancy. There are virtues that we find easy; others are difficult because they seem to be somewhat meaningless. To hope for what is not seen but remains hidden equally today as every day, yet keeps the same reality in God, to hope for what has little appeal to us because it does not come into our reach but is meant to keep us always in attention: this tires us. But we are not justified in giving in because of such tiredness, in withdrawing because of the invisibility, and keeping the virtue of hope for later days. Endurance is part of it, unchanging constancy. This constancy in us should correspond to the unchanging hope laid up in God. Our faith also is meant to be constant, but in faith we can shift the emphasis sometimes here and sometimes there, we can hold on with insight to the one and leave something else resting without touching on it, until its hour comes. But hope is indivisible, it is like a block that is equal in weight and pressure. Hope causes the same relief at every point, it is so one as to appear almost uniform; but this is necessary because we have need of it in this way, or even more because God expects it from us this way.

26. *Likewise the Spirit helps us in our weakness; for we do not know how to pray as we ought, but the Spirit himself intercedes for us with sighs too deep for words.*

The whole field of hope remains hidden. And the hope that is asked of us, and which inspires us, leaves us in our state of spirit and body: *in our weakness.* We hope in weakness. Hope itself is strong but we remain as we are. But God needs us to be strong. He wants us to be strong in faith, strong in love, strong in hope. So the Spirit comes to our aid, not where we are strong but where we are weak. We know that he lives in us, but he also shows us everything in its true light and rectifies our behavior in faith, hope and love. The Spirit of God, the Spirit of strength, *helps us in our weakness*. Not in order to underline the discrepancy; on the contrary, to overcome it, to put his strength in the place of our weakness. We are so weak that we do not even know what we need. The strong word of God's command wants us to be before him in prayer. We would like to pray, but we do not know *how to pray as we ought*. When we pray we are allowed to ask; as children of God we are allowed to ask that we may behave as children. But everything is so new, so large, so incomprehensible that we hardly find words and have forgotten the meaning and content of words. And even if we know what to pray for we would not know how to do it.

But we know what the Father expects from his Son and how the Son has prayed, and here we can entrust ourselves to the Spirit—as the Son entrusted himself to obedience—and regardless of our weakness the Spirit will ask rightly, led by his own insight, passing over our insight. But he does it *with sighs*, he behaves within us as one who is at home, and he does not spare us in prayer from anything. We need shaking up; we need sighs, sorrow. We cannot take refuge in our weakness in order to be spared. The Spirit of Strength who comes to our help is not an easygoing Spirit. He makes demands. Perhaps here and there he asks for something we ourselves would have wanted, but most often for what we would not have sought, what would have appeared unfitting to our own spirit. The Spirit of God asks God, and we are only located in between. The Spirit mediates and takes the initiative, because we in our weakness have entrusted ourselves to him. He takes up his dwelling in us not in appearance only: he is at home. And God listens to the Spirit because it is his Spirit. He recognizes his voice, even when we pray together with him, even when we say the words the Spirit inspires in us.

When the Spirit *intercedes for us* he intercedes for transformed beings, for those he represents, those who possess his strength, those who recognize suddenly what their prayer should be, as the Son presented himself before the Father on the Cross and bore the sins of the world. When the Son or the Spirit stand in on our behalf, they do so totally. No half-measures are possible for them. Our hesitations, our half-truths, our half-confessions find no room. They take us over so completely that they give us their own fullness. And now at last we understand that we cannot really pray in any other way than as driven by the Spirit, and that we can only suffer as suffering with the Son. Where we appeared to be at the end of our strength, that is, where our weakness reached its fullness, we may confide our insufficiency to the Son and the Spirit, that they may transform it into what is theirs, what can be heard and accepted by the Father. But then they have the right to dispose of us, spirit and body, as they think fit.

27.   *And he who searches the hearts of men knows what is the mind of the Spirit, because the Spirit intercedes for the saints according to the will of God.*

Repeatedly and from ever-different angles Paul shows us how the Triune God works in man. This work is immediate, but alongside and in between the acts of God and their effects in man there is the contemplation of what takes place in Heaven. There is a structure in the acts of God that allows us to have insight into something of its manner of working, to divine what God does together with God. God the Father *searches the hearts of men*. He knows them, penetrates into their ultimate depth and sees everything from the beginning, at this moment and for all the future. His knowledge does not become clouded over. Even should someone believe that in his hidden solitude he could reserve a thought to himself, or plan something or keep a secret from God, God is far better informed than he is himself. He disentangles the whole web of thoughts. But this knowledge of the heart of man in no wise intrudes on his knowledge of the Holy Spirit. He knows *what is the mind of the Spirit*, what he has done and intends to do; he knows it not only at the very instant but in the eternal interrelation of his eternal thoughts. And God recognizes himself in it. He is at home in the thoughts of the Spirit. This at-homeness is based on God's unity of being, but does not prevent any of the three Persons from acting in a personal way.

The Son says: Not my will be done, but Yours. In

this consent to the divine will he expresses his utter obedience, but also his knowledge of the Father's will. Similarly the Father knows the thoughts of the Spirit, and these thoughts are in accord with him. And when the Spirit intercedes for the saints, stands in for the believers and gives them in this representation something that brings them into accord with the Father, then this representation also corresponds to the Father's plan and will. There is no trace of contradiction or delay in submission or consent. What the Spirit demands and achieves is from the outset what the Father has known and desired. The believer knows himself held by the Spirit: on the one hand in himself, since the Spirit dwells in him and works in him as in his own house, on the other hand before the Father, since the Spirit puts him into his proper place before the Father and gives his faith the position the Father expects. This expectation expresses the faith and hope of man, and it also expresses the love of the Holy Spirit toward the Father's creatures, and finally the love of the Creator himself.

Love appears in this way not in a graduated form but made transparent for different levels and structures; for the Spirit is transparent before the Father, and the Son makes us transparent through his representation before the Father and enables us in this transparency given by him to understand the things of the Spirit. Were we expected to understand the life of the Son and his love and his sacrifice for us apart from the Spirit, we could not but humanize everything and take it out of the divine corelationship without which it cannot take effect. For the Son lives and dies in obedience to the Father as much as in the unity of Father and Son, a unity revealed through love, giving to this love the true perspective and the proper foundation. Only now we are able to learn in a Christian way in our attempts at loving, learn from our teacher, the Spirit, who represents us before God, who even represents God before God; which has no other purpose than that of revealing to us the living interplay of the being and the love of the Triune God.

IV

THE CERTAINTY

28. We know that in everything God works for good with those who love him, who are called according to his purpose.

Everything means there is no exception. It really means everything at all, not only the whole of creation or what man can imagine, but literally everything. This everything is not a confused heap of things, but interplay, a *working with*, nearby and at a distance, in things known and unknown. Perhaps man calls it his fate; he knocks against it, is annoyed or glad; according to his own thinking it interferes with his daily life or even alters his destiny. It has developed slowly and seemed to take a predictable course into which man has woven his own plans, but suddenly it changes direction and leaves in ruins all that went before. Or it remains vague from the outset, never deigning to reveal its face; it cannot be grasped as something desired or threatening. Man becomes fascinated by it, or he turns away from it and wants nothing to do with it. But however that may be, whatever stance a man may take to his fate, one thing is sure, that *God in everything works for good*. The fate has a definite purpose: the good of man. It is not merely a sum of facts. It has a definite meaning, it corresponds to a demand. Something is to come of it. The Apostle knows what this something is: it is the good of man.

Everything obeys a plan of God, who wants the best for man. God has made preparations; he has not only planned everything but also provided the possibilities that will make it happen. And what is happening is the good of man. Men are in relationship with all things because they *are called according to his purpose*, they are set apart and belong to this purpose, for the sake of which all other plans appear. They are the answer to the question that all things pose, or all things are the answer to the question that men themselves have to pose because they are called. The juxtaposition of all things with those who are called corresponds to a purpose, has been long foreseen and regulated, is on the verge of taking effect and working the good that is destined for man. We are now far removed from the moment of creation when a kind of dominion of man over everything in the world was initiated, and man perhaps had no idea yet what to do with the things of this world. For now it has become clear that all things exist in order to work together for his good, and it has also become apparent that even the hidden and incomprehensible things are not excluded from this cooperation. This relationship to man exists because he has been called. The order of man and that of created things do not exist merely alongside of each other, but are from the outset ordered toward each other in God's plan.

All things have been created for the Son; but everything, created or uncreated, works together for the good of man. Through this revelation man's position changes. The problem of his daily life, his plans, his responsibility and duty, his question about the meaning of life in general—all this has already received an answer. He has only to accommodate himself in such a way that he, too, together with all things, behaves according to the plan of God, recognizing in himself one who has been called, and in the light of this knowledge give the answer to all things and try to understand the world. Now he can be at peace as one who believes and is called. He is in his right place, and so is everything else. This does not permit him to be a quietist, but rather to act and pray joyfully at every moment of his life. He is allowed to contribute his share to the goodness of all things as they are. Through his faith and his following he is allowed to reveal the meaning of this good and present himself with everything he possesses and strives for in a joyful Yes.

29. For those whom he foreknew he also predestined to be conformed to the image of his Son, in order that he might be the firstborn among many brethren.

God did not create the world void of meaning. He has a plan for it, not a limited one but an eternal one. And all things have their place in his Holy Spirit. And since God is truth the world becomes a reality within his truth that cannot fall out of his plan, that is held secure by the Spirit. Thus integrated in the plan of God the world is not boring but alive. God's plan itself is life originating from the streaming life of the Triune God. Not in the sense that the world becomes equal to eternity, its finiteness equal to the infinity of Heaven, but in the sense that in his plan of the world from the beginning God the Father established relationships with the Son and the Spirit. The relations with the Son are living and effective already before the Son becomes man. Nothing in the world is left to chance for the world is alive in God's plan. He creates all things for the Son, therefore for men also, and these even in a privileged position. From the beginning they carry the image of God, and the long ages between the Fall and redemption did not blot out the purpose God had for them. God sees from the beginning *those whom he foreknew* and *he also predestined* them *to be conformed to the image of his Son.*

And in between the first image of creation and the image that is conformed to the Son, there is the living role of the Spirit, which in the predestination expresses itself in two ways: in God, when what he has eternally planned becomes suddenly and individually concrete and real, and in man, who is lifted to the purpose that God has for him. These two levels become one in the conformation to the image of the Son, as merit and grace penetrate each other to become one, or still better, action and contemplation,[1]

[1] Man is active in order to make contemplation possible, and contemplative to make action true. We need to differentiate between them because time is passing and not everyone can do

ever striving to become one in order to fulfill the will of God. If ever action and contemplation form a unity then it is in the Son. But the unity must be maintained by those who have been called in their following of him. And so the eternal plan of God and the present entering of the chosen into the realization of what has been eternally predestined have a common goal: to bring the chosen into conformity with the image of the Son. This image is not left to chance at the moment of realization; right from the beginning it has been directed toward the purpose *that he might be the firstborn among many brethren*, that he might not be alone and lost in the world, but find a home there through the Father's care and his eternal

---

everything. But the unity exists in the Lord as he shows us in his own life. It is at the same time an image of what occurs in Heaven, when certain actions—the creation of the world, the voice of the prophets, the mission of the Son—appear to us as active deeds of God, which he actively performs though otherwise all God's actions are enclosed in his contemplation. We ourselves have in the vision of God (the vision which God has of us) our place within the Son's work of redemption and the Father's plan of creation, who created us for the greater glory of the Triune God. Whether we understand and occupy our place already today as those in eternity do or whether only at the end of our earthly days, it is always in existence, for we belong to the contemplation of God. God's action cannot be separated from his contemplation because it contains the rich fullness of God, but it sends forth like radiant flashes of lightning knowledge destined for us, so that we may recognize God's presence in his action as in his contemplation.

plan. If Adam was not an outcast in paradise, this was because the voice of God accompanied him and because God had created the world so that he might find his place in it. But this took place so that the first man should live in expectation of the others who would come after, for in Eve already he recognized what he had been waiting for. The second Adam, too, was meant to recognize his brethren in those predestined by the Father, he was not meant to be alone in his move from Heaven to earth and back to Heaven but accompanied by chosen ones who in the plan of God are eternally destined to take part in his movement as a fitting escort to the Son: fitting because the call to be chosen obliges.

In this way the different levels and aspects can be sorted out in order to arrive more easily at the unity: of time, of space, of creation, redemption, in order for each image to be completed by the others, until everything is welded together into the plan of God, and the Son receives the necessary companionship; until the will of God that the Son alone is able to fulfill will also be fulfilled in the others. Through their predestination they are not only able but empowered and called to this in the same way as the Son, not through their merit, but through the grace of predestination; as something that was planned by the Father and is not meant for individual men as such but for the Son. This gives a new face to holiness. The saints are not holy and do not do the will of God by their own strength or in order to be regarded as especially chosen and perfect, but in order to be a gift for the Son. The shining figure is the Son. Everything else in the world and among men remains anonymous until it receives a name in the Son, the name: brethren, so that the Son with his brethren together can address God as "Father". There is nothing here of aloneness, individualism, nothing even of personal freedom of the Son to call; everything is obedience, will and plan of the Father from eternity. It is from there we have to consider not only the way of the Son but also that of the Church, secure in the Father to the very end, willed by the Father in this and no other way, blessed by the Father from within its predestination.

30. *And those whom he predestined he also called; and those whom he called he also justified; and those whom he justified he also glorified.*

There is no gap anywhere in God's plan. Every person has his place in it, and every road has already been brought to its goal in God, merely through a man's creation and his redemption by the Son. *Those whom he predestined he also called.* Therefore they hear his voice and perceive the call: they are predestined to know the voice of God and follow it. This does not exclude the necessity of great vigilance, even because of the very fact of being predestined; they have to contribute by their consent to the design of God. They can give this consent only as response after having received the call. So man cannot believe himself to be an outcast, abandoned, left alone, reserved to an unknown destiny. He is on the way. Did not Christ say of himself that he is the Way? All things that have been created for the Son meet again at this point. All that has been predestined is called to the Way, called by the way toward him, the individual and the whole, orienting itself toward the Lord and belonging to the Church. This belonging to the Church is part of the plan of God from eternity, and here all men find the house by the wayside, the support and the help they may look for. The Church is visible and invisible at the same time; the believer sees in the invisible the visible, in the Catholic concept of the House of God the material one, this house by the wayside where he is at home before God, even with God. His being created for something receives here its final concretization: in the adoration of the Host, in prayer before the tabernacle, in remaining within the house built by the hand of man for the glory of God. Everything he knows about houses in his experience and through tradition he can find confirmed in the House of God; the most peripheral things: resting, eating, thinking and planning, where the two levels of the human and divine dimension touch each other, where the visible Host makes the invisible God present. Whoever dwells here is called; called because predestined, called such as he is, with all the horizons that offer themselves to him, called in readiness but also in the fulfillment of that which he has to achieve through the Lord.

And those whom he called he also justified. Justified

we are in the Son, so that the vocation now enlarges and takes on the shape of the Lord's achievement: the shape of the Incarnation, of his Cross, of his being the Word and the wonder-worker, of his Ascension. It is an encounter one would have to describe almost in physical terms: our sinful blood meets his sacrificial blood; the pain we impose on the world meets his acceptance of this pain in his suffering. It is an encounter of the Lord with every sinner for the sake of justifying him, so that what the Father foresaw may become reality. And we become, again in the Church, as people whom the Lord's blood has justified, a holy community, because what counts is no longer our own individual being and doing but the Lord's being and doing that has brought about our justification, is at work in it, reveals it, makes it effective. Nobody is justified for himself alone but for the community, together with the community for the Lord, so that his way constantly points back to his being created for the Son, but also to the Cross, including the present moment and leading ahead to eternity. This means that all time—past, present and future—meets together in our justification by the eternal Son at each moment, from the moment when the Incarnation was decreed, and still further back from the moment of creation, until the end of the world.

And those whom he justified he also glorified. Justification again is not an act that has its end in itself. What would it be to us to be justified? It would be a state similar to that of an accused man against whom nothing can be proved, who is acquitted of his guilt, whose behavior can at most be allowed to pass, without the acts of the process yielding any more than his innocence in this particular case. He had a valid reason for being present at the scene of the crime; he is unlikely to have committed it, or he cannot have done it at all; perhaps the criminal has already been found. Justification by God is something quite different, corresponding to predestination and leading by the shortest route to glorification. The justified man is glorified; that means he can take his place very close to the Lord and see in this place the summary of all his earthly life. He was a man in order to glorify God, to contribute to his glory and receive a share in it. He was meant to live in love for God, but this love is so weighty that it cannot be accomplished in passing time; the longest life would not be long enough, eternity is necessary to give it its meaning. And the meaning God wishes to give it is glorification for all future eternity, and for all past eternity, because love participates in the eternal predestination by the Father. Every eternity occurs anew in man, finds a fulfillment in every present moment of the here or the hereafter because predestination leads through vocation and justification to glorification, because the way is marked and each of its stages and because everything has been gathered together by the word of the Apostle and gathered in by the Church. For the Church also finds herself in this word and remains the Bride of the Lord, the Bride of whom we are part, the Bride whom the Lord created as institution by adapting her to the need of his Word and whom he makes the place of its realization: Church now suddenly as mirror, as receiver, as focal point of all Christian words, put together in such a way that the Lord sees himself in her entirely and reveals through her to men the intentions of the Father and heavenly life.

Predestination means the eternity that precedes, glorification the eternity that follows after, vocation and justification the moment in time in which all moments meet and come together, because we have been called and justified not in ourselves but in the Son who comes from eternity and goes into eternity. And the concrete place of it all, the house where all this takes place, is the Church, in the same way as a kiss given is the proof of love.

31.   What then shall we say to this? If God is for us, who is against us?

Paul is not asking a rhetorical question. He puts in a breathing space, a moment of silence between the enormity of what he has just said and of what he is going to say next. He will draw two consequences: for the world and for today, from eternity. He will not concern himself with the temporal and worldly, with everyday worries; his thoughts are occupied with the relationship of Heaven to earth, eternity to mortality, God to man. And he wants to produce an effect in the life of Christians by his statements. It is the task of Christians to create from everyday realities something that makes the Spirit of God visible; that will be a sign; he is to make his deeds significant for others through his own prayer- and faith-experience.

The encounter between the here and the hereafter is to take place in the believer himself, in his smallest deed, but also in every prayer. The measure of his hope should be that of his love, and people should be able to read in his lived attitude of love what it is that distinguishes the Christian from other men, a real distinction. However the Christian cannot be transparent on this point to everyone. He is transparent to God because God has given this transparency to him: but, for the unbeliever he has a new form of opaqueness that makes him appear questionable. That is why Paul now looks for another principle of distinction that leaves room for an opponent, an outsider, so that a new light may fall from outside on what from within is seen as closeness to God.

If God is for us who is against us? That God is for us means the commitment, the new obligation, a closeness of relationship that creates, strengthens and nourishes faith and is its source and overflow. The *who* that stands against this closeness is already weakened by the question, devalued, unimportant, without relevance. Relevance lies in God, given by him and dependent on him. The opposing *who* has no name and no effect; his power—however important it may appear to the unbeliever—has no further effect on the believer, for *God is for us*. The *for* is a *for* of eternity, which can become effective anywhere. Its mere existence suffices: God is for us! God says Yes to our attitude, God supports our attempts with his love, God throws something of his eternity, infinity and power onto our side of the scales. God declares himself for us from eternity, and this declaration has the effect that we can live with confidence and are enabled to make this important statement against anyone who might be against us. And the Christian way and the Church and the whole life in faith are part of what Paul means when he says: *God is for us*.

32. *He who did not spare his own Son but gave him up for us all, will he not also give us all things with him?*

In God's deed of love every love is contained: everything we feel to be love, but beyond that also everything that we human beings would never be able to include in the concept of love. God, who did not spare his own Son, has done a deed that we find difficult to read as love. We try to imagine the Divine Persons and attribute to them everything we understand as love and which for the most part is softness, spoiling, inability on our part to endure the sufferings of others. But God did not spare his Son *but gave him up for us all*. For love of us he did something that we could never interpret as love, for love spares. The Father, however, not only did not spare the Son, he handed him over, turned away from him, betrayed him and cast him out into loneliness, allowed him to die in forsakenness. The cry on the Cross gives witness to this abandonment. And the whole is the sign of love for us who are unworthy, who do not understand it at all, who are weak in faith and in deeds of faith.

What betrayal is we know from the threefold denial of Peter. What he did appears so unworthy to our weak faith, so against every love, so hateful, that we want to dissociate ourselves from it in every way, that we want to obliterate in our language the words "to hand over", "to deny", "to betray". But now the Father himself has handed over, and his own Son. And the Son has from the beginning given his consent. He became man in order to be the one handed over. He has loved the Father so much that he expected from the Father's love nothing else but to be handed over. And at the last opportunity when to be spared still would have been possible, he asks the Father that his will may be done. Here the Cross receives through this word of handing over, betrayal, ruthlessness, a meaning that is beyond us. It becomes a matter between Father and Son; and we are the ones at stake, in whose favor the Father acts, seemingly setting aside the Son. The Father says Yes to us and No to the Son. He spares us, he keeps us near to himself; the Son he unsparingly hands over, as though he valued our love more than that of his Son, as if our endurance and value meant more to him.

Paul uses this image from human experience to explain to us the intentions of God. God did not hand his Son over for nothing or treat him badly without an end in view. Everything was tending toward us; in the same way in which all things were created for the Son, the Son now is handed over with us in view, is given for us. But the gift comes into sight accompanied by all the things that the Father gives us together with his Son. His most precious treasure, the perfect love of the Son, he gives to us, and the Son feels abandoned; but we know that he is accompanied by all the things that the Father designs to make over to us and pours out in front of us.

At creation all things were created for the Son, but the Son as goal was not yet visible. Man saw the things God had created—plants, animals, himself—and he had to conclude that there was a direction without having seen the goal, the Son himself. Now we know the Son; we really have experienced in faith what love is and what God is; we see him hanging naked on the Cross, dying for us, under the burden of each of our sins. And we must know that his forsakenness is surrounded and accompanied by everything that the Father destines for us. We are not condemned to see the Son die only under the burden of sin, but also under the burden of everything the Father means us to have. He is overwhelmed by it all, so to say, and what oppresses and suffocates him, what is meant for us, has nothing to do with him, the Father has decided it. These are the things that he wants to give us sometime, perhaps now, perhaps tomorrow or much later, or which maybe he has given us already long ago for love of us. And it is as if the Father is constantly compelled to add more to it, everything we might think of, whatever we need, whatever can serve to make our faith easier, strengthen our hope, vivify our love. And the Son stands beside all this as one minimized, unimportant, because the Father wants to give everything, and the betrayal of the Son and his unsparing treatment have become side issues. The weight lies on love for us. This enormous statement of Saint Paul must appear incredible to his hearers. But this absence of credibility, this outrageous line of thought, linked up with the reality of the Cross and the handing over of the Son, gives us suddenly a faint idea of what love is. All our imaginations, all that we put together in our pitiful attempt to love, this and something else or more that seems to us to deserve the name of love, proves itself to be wholly inadequate, hardly points in the right direction in which the Father's essential love is to be found, which is at the same time the essence of Triune love.

33-34a. Who shall bring any charge against God's elect? It is God who justifies; who is to condemn?

The elect now form a unity made real in the Church; its measure is determined by belonging to and being related to the Church. The unity is, however, still in a place inaccessible to us; we know only that it exists in God, in the place of his design, of his prediction and plan. The elect are part of it long before their existence, before they know anything of their Christianity. The mature Christian knows in faith about his relationship to God; he knows the distance, in prayer he knows him as partner. "Here" he adores his God who is "there". Here he lives his everyday life, surrounded by believers and unbelievers—and there the Son is sitting at the Father's right hand. Here he is himself with his questions and troubles and all that belongs to human life, all that occupies him, with his difficulties of today and tomorrow—and there everything is already solved for him, inserted into the plan of God. Here he forms with believers—many of whom he knows and others whom he will never know—a group called God's elect, but he cannot say anything about their number or their interior life; perhaps he has a limited insight into the soul of another, but he cannot penetrate and experience it or make a judgment of it. In that place everything is already now included in God, every one of those who have been chosen with him, each with his destiny, with his life in faith, is included with him in God, and the link formed by this inclusion is the closest one can imagine. Every moment the elect can knock at God's door with a petition, a sigh; everything is prepared to receive him and include him in what has already long been predicted. His knocking is an answer in itself, which he gives because it was long expected; what God has planned happens at the right moment. The Christian is a part of what God wants to make real. However lonely and tempted, deserted and misunderstood he may feel himself to be in the world, he dwells in God's providence, in his predestination; the earthly, worldly, everyday aspects lose their sharpness, value and immediacy, for his actuality is in God. But God has nevertheless entrusted him with a task; he is not in the world for nothing, he may not withdraw from what is waiting for him.

And so it happens that he is accused by others, tried and misunderstood. But *who shall bring any charge against God's elect?* That he is chosen means that his actions take place within a justification coming from God, and so nobody can condemn him. He is situated in a today that loses and gains its weight at the same time: the values in which he lives are different from those of his fellow man; he receives the blows of fate but also its favors more calmly, if not at the moment, yet in retrospect. He experiences a joy and knows a greater one. He suffers a pain, but his suffering is changed in several respects: it is allowed by God, so it is right that he should suffer; he may offer his suffering as a share in the Lord's suffering, and he knows about this greater suffering. Finally, this suffering has a meaning not only for himself but also for the Church, and can promote his prayer, his faith, his Christian maturity. So there is a gain in the loss because everything is for God, and as one of the elect he is so totally on the way to God that in accepting what has been allowed, he enters more deeply into the meaning of it, into the meaning of every reparation, every suffering at all.

34b. Is it Christ Jesus, who died, yes, who was raised from the dead, who is at the right hand of God, who indeed intercedes for us?

The more profound reason for the words of Paul follows; it begins abruptly. *Christ Jesus died.* The short statement expresses the greatness of the sacrifice, not only of the Son but also of the Father and the Spirit. Death is the punishment of sin, and the Son suffers this punishment. But there is more: *Yes, who was raised from the dead.* Out of death and punishment new life, new grace has come, grace out of punishment, life out of death. The grain of wheat died to bear fruit, and the fruit was the Resurrection. The disciples saw the Son ascend to Heaven, they participated bodily in this grace, were left behind gifted with a new promise: to expect the Spirit from Heaven. The grace of his death consisted in their being made capable of knowing him as Lord in Heaven; the concrete experience of the risen Lord makes them capable of receiving the Spirit. And the Son is *at the right hand of God* the Father. That is his place, and he does the one thing: *He indeed intercedes for us.* When contemplating in prayer what has become of the Lord through death and Resurrection—the word of Paul tells us: he has become the Intercessor—he never tires of standing before God on our behalf. His prayer receives a new dimension in our eyes: it is the prayer of the one who is sure to be heard; he has suffered and died, he has achieved the whole work in order to offer the Father the atonement for our sin.

The Son does not turn away from us, he does not leave us behind in uncertainty, or merely with the promise of the Cross or with the grace given to the Church: he takes part. He continues, and his part is prayer. This makes our prayer suddenly come to life, for in prayer we do nothing else but what the Son does; we do it in our weakness, but supported by his infallibility. The prayer for the world, for the Church, for humanity is prayer of the Son in which we are allowed to share. We stand there as people who pray without doing anything of ourselves, but praying together with the Son who takes into his prayer all his work achieved, and we through prayer may share in his sacrifice. If we have been created for the Son, this new word of Paul confirms the meaning of creation: to be participation in the work of Christ. We were created for him, but now we have become cosharers in his prayer; he takes over the whole greatness of prayer, the perfect conversation with the Father, he gives it the divine meaning of his intercession and invites us to pray with him. And while praying together with him we recognize the weakness of those who accuse and condemn us. For the Lord prays for the world, also for those who accuse; and he has offered himself for all in order to be able to intercede in this way, at the right hand of God and yet not separated from those who are his own. Through the Cross he has gained the right to mark his own in such a way that they are signed with his sign, are his co-pray-ers.

35. Who shall separate us from the love of Christ? Shall tribulation, or distress, or persecution, or famine, or nakedness, or peril, or sword?

If we are the elect from all eternity, we were so before we were born, in the love of God. And there was a long time in our existence—before we awoke to our Christianity—when we were fully enclosed in the love of God, so entirely that no one could see us. Who could say anything about a saint or prophet or believer who lives in God's plan, who is among the elect today and has been so for a long time but who will appear on earth only a hundred years hence? Unnumbered are those who are thus hidden in the love of God while God in his providence already now prepares a way for them and takes part in their future work. The believers whom Paul addresses are in the love of God, but they have always been in it, for they cannot be separated from it. Love encloses them and exposes them at the same time, because they are visible in the world, because they struggle and are tested. This visibility is not a dismissal from love, but rather a kind of coming of age, a vulnerability that belongs to the Cross. The Christian must suffer, but in suffering he is not separated from the love of God. Paul mentions all the powers that may fill with fear someone who is discouraged, the fear that these powers might be strong enough to cause a separation, as though *distress* were a power capable of taking up battle against God, and the others equally so, as if someone had reason to feel he was being handed over to these powers.

But the Son, himself, was he not also handed over? As soon as this connection appears, the thought of being handed over receives its Christian face. The believer knows that even on the Cross the Son was not separated from the Father's love, that no tribulation, distress, or persecution or whatever else it might be, can separate from love; on the contrary, here lies the very proof that we are enclosed in the Father's love. On the Cross love showed itself even stronger the stronger temptation became. And the Father handed the Son over only to show his love, not only his love for the Person of the Son, but his love for all men embraced by the Son's love. The friends of our friends are our friends; among men this paying is a truism, in God a sublime truth, for the Father truly loves those loved by the Son. And the Son loves those whom the Father has chosen. Love dares to do things like handing over and being forsaken, not only in order to prove itself, but to bring about the redemption of the beloved ones, in order to be able to extend the Son's intercession at the right hand of God to all.

When Paul speaks of *tribulation, distress or persecution* he mentions matters known to the Son and which we get to know in a new way through him. But we also know them from human experience, as things that hurt and haunt our life and appear to us incomprehensible and more oppressive than we feel we can bear. But we cannot separate them from the sufferings of the Lord. He has suffered them and made them Christian, so that in all their harshness they appear as powerless, for behind them shines the Father's love for the Son and the Triune love for men. Anyone who has suffered anguish knows how inexorable it can be and what a world of mysteries it conjures up before our eyes. He hates it because it makes him distressed and powerless, but he must nonetheless love it because it is not his own anguish but belongs to that of the Lord. He suddenly loves what he wants to avoid and cannot but hate, he loves it because his hatred is not strong enough to hold out against love; his hatred has been overcome on the Cross of the Lord, and his weakness enters immediately into the weakness of the Lord.

Paul goes on to mention *famine, nakedness, peril and sword*. These are earthly things that are imaginable to everyone. But famine can also be the Lord's thirst on the Cross, nakedness his nakedness. Peril can be his hanging on the Cross, and sword the lance that transpierced him. There is none of these life-threatening powers that he does not know from his Passion. But the cool consideration of his Passion and a faith merely noticing the reality without being able to imagine it, is something different from contemplating it as an experience of the Lord, shared with us in what we ourselves are experiencing. Contemplative prayer receives here a new urgency, the words of Paul are words of reality and of contemplation at the same time. The early Christians knew what persecution and famine could be, but even more than from their own experience they knew it from the experience of the life of Christ. Their being threatened from outside awakened this knowledge to new actuality. They were able to entrust their own small anguish to his great nameless one, their peril to his death. Their small concern disappears before the much greater one in him.

36.   As it is written: "For thy sake we are being killed all the day long; we are regarded as sheep to be slaughtered".

Now it is no longer the relationship only of the personal fate of the individual Christian with the Lord's Passion, nor the present time only, but an actuality reaching back into the Old Covenant. From the fulfillment we look back to the promise. *For thy sake we are being killed all the day long.* This death has a foundation that is the Lord. Because he was persecuted and died on the Cross, we are persecuted and killed all the day long. The expression is not exaggerated, for the Christian is for evermore exposed to the malice of the world, just as the Lord was exposed not only at the hour of his death but from his birth. The innocent children belong to the picture, as signs on the way of the Lord. Jesus was the first martyr, and before the disciples became martyrs the children take their place. The martyrdom lasts all the day long, without interruption.

We are regarded, counted, valued *as sheep to be*

slaughtered. A counterimage to the eternal election by the Father. The election is mirrored in the judgment of the world, in the election to the slaughter. In this way Paul points out the rightness of the Christian way, understood not merely as personal destiny but as a service counted on, which has its appointed place: service to the Lord, fulfillment of an expectation of the Lord, answer to his word. At the same time there is a line of truth that can be followed through the whole of Scripture leading to the threat of today and to a security and grace for those who experience it. If martyrs died with a smile on their lips, it is because they were animated by a certainty that is sheer grace, promised in the Old Covenant and made true during the whole time of the New; entry of Heaven into earthly reality, influence of the beyond on the level of the here and now, completion of the Lord's way by those eternally predestined with him. The way belongs to the Lord. But even in his abandonment, even in his cry on the Cross he makes room and opens the way for his brothers and followers.

37. No, in all these things we are more than conquerors through him who loved us.

We here admit that we can do nothing of our own strength, but everything through the Spirit of love and through him who loves us. The image of man is totally transformed, we are far removed from a battle like that between David and Goliath; there are no forces that can be measured against each other, no battle where those smaller in numbers gain the victory over the stronger. Nor is it a unique act of the heavenly Father infusing courage and strength into us; we stand there merely as servants, in readiness for service. And the Lord not only asks us for service but also guarantees the success. His giving and demanding are so inextricably bound up with each other that it would be labor lost to try and separate them. Just as we have been predestined by the Father from eternity and have been shown the way, we are more than conquerors, victorious in every difficulty and against every threat. Here we see what divine love truly is. It is everything. Not everything in a random fulfillment of all wishes and successes; but differentiated in the life of each one who experiences it and has a share in it.

We are more than conquerors. The Spirit of love knows no stinting, but is lavish beyond every need. The success is adequate and at the same time superabundant, because the strength is sufficient, and more strength was at our disposal than we needed. It is the same superabundance as on the Cross where everything that sinners could not expect was included in what they did expect; what could be counted, examined and measured contained there everything they never had any idea of: the hidden in what is revealed. We see how the Lord gives his garments and they are taken, he gives his freedom and is nailed; we finally see his death. But in between these events we can follow, everything is contained that is hidden in his words and also everything that was never uttered and remains within the intimacy of the life he shares with the Father. He gives us the same superabundance in our victory. Perhaps we know where we have been conquerors over the sword or hunger, or persecution. But there are many victories that we have won without having any idea of it; with astonishment we would have to agree if God were to show them to us. But God does not count them, and this should be a lesson for us: our spirit also must learn not to count. It comes natural to us to count. We are easily content with small victories, or even with an undecisive result, and of ourselves we would be ready for many compromises. So we are amazed to find ourselves, who are always weak, to be always conquerors.

But there is no need to understand everything. And the Lord is capable of giving us the place of conquerors where we ourselves thought we were not even present, because he has loved us so much that he loves not only the individual and the community as such, but the Father's cause and the cause of the Church which is ever greater, which is eternal within our futility. That is how true love acts. If we meditate on this it will make us want to shout out how trivial our own love is and how it fails, but that is not asked of us exactly at this moment; we are asked to recognize the victory which is that of love and to open our heart and our faith anew to love.

38-39. For I am sure that neither death, nor life, nor angels, nor principalities, nor things present, nor things to come, nor powers, nor height, nor depth, nor anything else in all creation, will be able to separate us from the love of God in Christ Jesus our Lord.

He who has loved us gives us the victory through his love's constant abiding with us. We do not do something in a given place that leads to victory so that we then experience that God has helped us to win this victory from some other place of his own. Through his love God is what is living and acting in us. Nor can his presence be understood as if with one part of himself he lived in this person and with a different part in another. God is everywhere perfectly present, divinely present, present in love, and nothing can separate us from him. Paul counts up many powers that might be able to effect a separation; powers arranged in battle against us and against God, with all manner of names. To prevent us becoming accustomed to one single concept representing the enemy, Paul calls upon every *height* and every *depth* to trip up our arithmetic. We cannot say: one *power* of such and such a size will not conquer us, but in double or tenfold strength it could become dangerous. Or: the greatest *power* cannot put us to the test today, but if it lasts longer we cannot guarantee the victory.

Next to height and depth he places *things present* and *things to come*. Our mind is confronted with every possibility that could provide an objection.

Finally everything is included: *anything else in all creation*. Whatever can be called "creature", whether loved or hated by us, expected or suppressed, powerful or weak, in permanent resistance or attacking only once: it cannot prevent the victory. Our imagination can try to represent to itself everything possible, God's imagination, which is to say, the power of his love, is stronger. But because everything in God is love, because he lives in us as love, and his love in us is always the expression of Triune Love—love of the Father for our Lord, love of the Spirit for him, love of the Son for the Father and Spirit—because of this everything we can try to imagine this love to be, lags far behind the reality. In actuality, everything is different, bigger and more effective; so effective that the Apostle not merely suspects this, he *is sure*. This certainty comes from God and is part of his love; for it would not be enough if God always gave us the victory without granting us who belong to him this certainty of being victors. In this certainty all to whom the words of Paul are addressed can say Yes to every task given by God, and embrace every covenant he offers. The victory belongs to them, is theirs, a tremendous victory, willed and guaranteed by God: the victory of Love.